TOO GOOD A GIRL

REMEMBERING OLENE EMBERTON
AND THE MYSTERY OF HER DEATH

WITHDRAWN

TOO GOOD A GIRL

REMEMBERING OLENE EMBERTON
AND THE MYSTERY OF HER DEATH

JANIS THORNTON

LIFE SENTENCES PUBLISHING

All rights reserved. No part of this book may be used or reproduced in any form or by any electronic or mechanical means without permission in writing from the publisher, except for brief quotations for use in a review, article, or blog. Contact Life Sentences Publishing LLC for more information.

Although the author and publisher have made every effort to ensure the accuracy and completeness of information contained in this book, they assume no responsibility for errors, inaccuracies, omissions, or any inconsistency herein. In addition, they disclaim any liability in connection with the use of this book.

©2018 by Janis Thornton

Published in the United States by Life Sentences Publishing LLC, Tipton, Indiana, *www.lifesentencespublishing.com*.

Printed in the United States of America.

ISBN: 978-0-692-15115-0

Cover and interior design by Janis Thornton.
Author photo by Christy Clark.

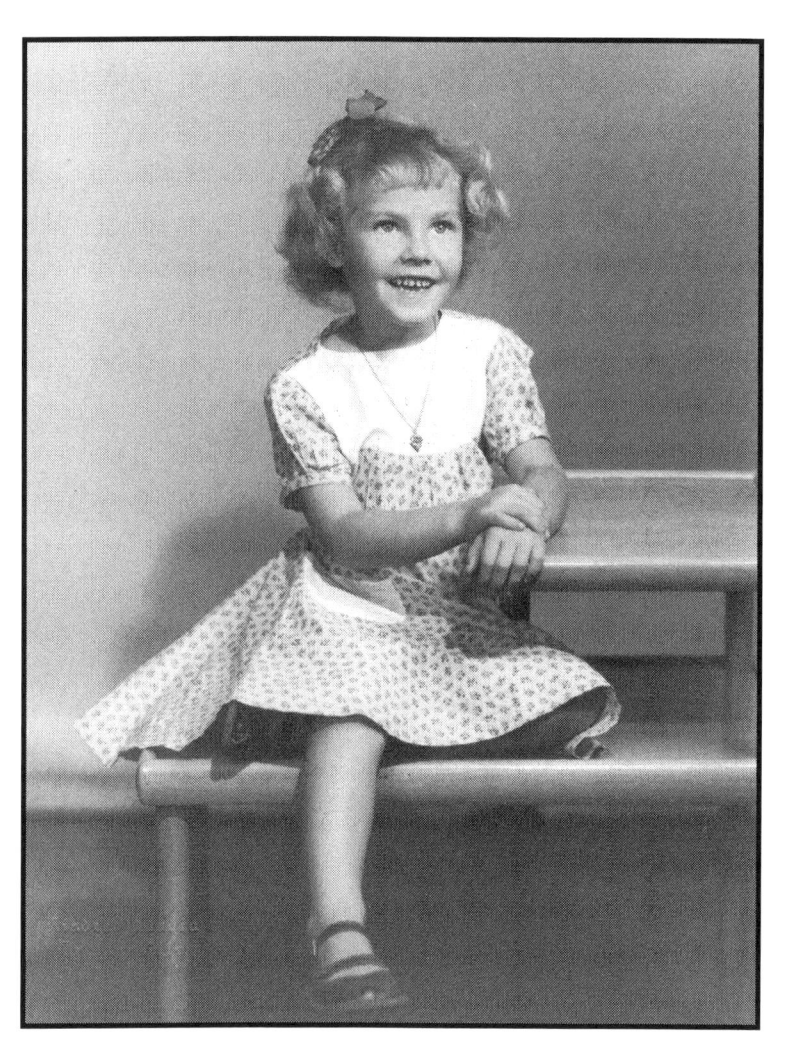

"Olene was too good a girl to have to face death this way."

— Roxie Emberton
As told to the *Kokomo Tribune*
November 24, 1965

Dedication

For Floyd and Roxie, who never gave up

Table of Contents

Dedication vi
Acknowledgements ix
Foreword by Mayor Don Havens xi
Foreword by Former Tipton High School Principal Charles Edwards xiii
Introduction xv
Chapter 1 • Author's Point of View:
               The Day Something Iniquitous Blew Into Town 1
Chapter 2 • Lost and Found 5
Chapter 3 • Saturday: Dawn to Doom 7
Chapter 4 • Author's Point of View: Analyses of the Crime Scene 14
Chapter 5 • Hope to Heartache 22
Chapter 6 • Who was Olene Emberton? 29
Chapter 7 • The Emberton Family 37
Chapter 8 • Shock Rocks Tipton 48
Chapter 9 • The Long Walk to Goodbye 54
Chapter 10 • Author's Point of View: The Viewing 61
Chapter 11 • Meanwhile, Back at the Jail 64
Chapter 12 • Brick Wall 68

Chapter 13 • Who Was Verl Grimme? 74
Chapter 14 • Rumor Mill 87
Chapter 15 • Who Was Tom Preston? 97
Chapter 16 • Author's Point of View: The Tom Preston I Remember 106
Chapter 17 • Pinkerton to the Rescue 112
Chapter 18 • Reward 125
Chapter 19 • A Viable Suspect Emerges 128
Chapter 20 • Author's Point of View: Nine Minutes 142
Chapter 21 • Anniversary Remembrances 150
Chapter 22 • Final Thoughts 153
Chapter 23 • Epilogue: Murder or Misdemeanor 157
Diagrams Tipton & Tipton County Noting Relevant Locations 160
Timeline 162
Who's Who 167
Bibliography 172
Index 179

Acknowledgements

Thank you, Debbie Emberton (wife of Olene's brother, David), for your trust and blessing. If not for you, I would never have resumed and finished this project. Furthermore, thank you for lending me precious family photos and original, confidential documents, which contained details about the case that were unavailable through any other source. For all of this, and your friendship, too, I will be forever grateful.

Much gratitude is also extended to the following individuals for their invaluable information, assistance, and contributions:

Members of the Tipton High School Class of 1966
Wanda Cherry Abney, Ed Achenbach, Bill Brackney, Patricia Scott Brooks, Karen Sottong Brown, Jennifer Wiggins Cels, Mary Neal Coan, Terry Conwell, Alice Pitcher Cummins, Jill Kinder Edgar, Sharon Bronson Foland, Jim Harmon, Randy Horton, Shirley Stewart Huss, Dixie McNew Ihnat, Marijane Fakes Jay, Sandy McCullough Lewis, Dennis Murray, John O'Banion, Linda Stewart Peters, Vickie Sallee Porter, Jo Anna Weber Powell, Ann Cain Reeves, Karen Burk Ripberger, Karyn Harkness Roseberry, Phil Roudebush, Floetta McAdams Scelta, Bill Tidler, Marla Henderson Wittkamper, and Gail Purdue Wix.

Members of local and state law enforcement agencies
Former Indiana State Police Officers Jim Bradley, Michael Colgate, Dick Hart and Robert Zell; former Director of the Indiana State Police Crime Lab Major Justus Littlejohn; former Tipton Police Chief Jim Pratt; former Tipton County Coroner Phil Nichols; current Tipton County Coroner Brad Nichols; Tipton County Deputy Sheriff, Major Mike Tarrh; and former Howard County Sheriff Marshall "Marty" Talbert.

Members and former members of the city and county of Tipton
Former Tipton Mayor David Berkemeier, Neal Curry, former Tipton High School Principal Charles Edwards, Matt Geas, Anna Gipson, Beryl Grimme, Mayor Don Havens, Diane Grimme Henderson, Doris Morris, Keith Porter, Margie Porter, Mollie Reecer Russell, and Joe Watson.

Others
Tim Bath, Bob Beilouny, Tim Byers, Dr. Robert Forney Jr., Marcy Fry, Ruth Illges, Nicole Kobrowski, Tom Kohlmeier, Jeff Kovaleski, J.D. "Chip" Mann, Mary Marlow, Bob Nash, Larry Sells, and Kathy Smith.

Foreword

BY TIPTON MAYOR DON HAVENS

It has been fifty-three years since the author and the subject were Tipton High School classmates and friends. It has been fifty-three years since Olene Emberton's body was found peacefully resting alongside a Tipton County road. What happened to Olene was going to be Tipton's mystery of the year. It has become the mystery of the past fifty-three years.

Author Janis Thornton captures the essence of the mystery in this story of small-town America and the impact of the death of one of its young members. The story is well-written and the read is quick, especially to those who have some memory of the event.

1965 in rural Indiana was a time of natural simplicity. The Vietnam War was thousands of miles away and the draft was four years away. Doors to homes were not locked at night, and keys were left in the family car. Kids of all ages felt safe and secure, and their school and friends were a warm cocoon.

On the night of October 16, a Saturday, Olene didn't come home to her family. At Tipton High School on October 18, a Monday, the author and her friends and classmates knew of Olene's disappearance and feared the worst because she was "Too Good a Girl."

This true account of those days is limited only by the two unknown truths: who was Olene with and how did she die? Janis Thornton takes us through the entire cast of characters, their known thoughts and actions, and the dilemma of mystery.

This foreword is being written in 2018 by me as the mayor of Tipton. In 1966, as a reporter for the *Kokomo Morning Times*, I wrote the anniversary story regarding Olene's mysterious death. I remember that time well, and I can attest that Janis, in the pages that follow, provides a read that will provoke memories and questions among those who lived, and about those who died, with knowledge of Olene and her untimely death.

Don Havens
Mayor, Tipton, Indiana

Foreword

BY FORMER TIPTON HIGH SCHOOL PRINCIPAL CHARLES EDWARDS

I served as principal for Tipton High School from 1965 through 1974, and during those years, nothing was as challenging as helping our students get through the hours, days, weeks, and months that followed Olene Emberton's devastating death.

I remember Olene as a cooperative and respectful student. When I learned Sunday, October 17 that she hadn't come home after a Saturday night date, it seemed out of character for the girl I knew.

Nothing could have prepared me for the phone call I received Monday afternoon from Sheriff Grimme: "We found the Emberton girl, and, oh, Charlie, she's dead." I immediately called the faculty together and began planning how we would tell the students.

I went to see the Embertons that evening. Olene's aunt, Olean Jackson, was there, and she told me, "Mr. Edwards, I got down on my knees and prayed that if she was dead, they find the body and bring this to an end. Her family couldn't bear the anguish of not knowing."

As the school's principal, I had to deal with the students' emotional loss, and more importantly, their physical security. I had to take my emotions out of it. But when I went home, I took off that administrator's hat and felt the sorrow of it all. In addition, I was worried about the safety of my wife and kids. Brook was fourteen, and Jill was nine. No one knew what had happened. Olene was a fine young person, and her life was taken. You had to wonder who would be next.

When Janis Thornton contacted me this spring to tell me she was writing about Olene's death, I was apprehensive about the wisdom of stirring up the past. More than fifty years had gone by, and I had pushed the sad incident from my mind. However, after reading Janis' thought-provoking book, the memories are vivid again, and I appreciate her efforts in documenting and weaving together the strands of this terrible chapter in Tipton's history.

Charles Edwards
Former Principal of Tipton High School

Introduction

The year was 1965, and throughout America, sweeping changes were underway. America's identity was being redefined by a profusion of shocking events — the bombing of the 16th Street Baptist Church, the assassination of President Kennedy, and the growing intensity and fear mongering of the Cold War among them. The country's deepening military presence in Southeast Asia was increasing the loss of life, and fear of repercussion was seeping into every demographic of society. Malcontents labeled the unrest a natural evolution, while others saw revolution. A counterculture of young people was shaking up the status quo and challenging the establishment to care for its own, protect the planet, and make love, not war.

Tipton, my Midwestern hometown — population 6,000, situated on the buckle of the biscuits and sausage-gravy belt of rich, Central Indiana farmland — certainly wasn't isolated from the woes that plagued the nation. We had other priorities. Our lives were deeply rooted in the community, revolving around God, Main Street, our families, and high school basketball. We loved our 4H fairs, homecoming parades, Blue Devil sundaes, tenderloins at Six Acres Drive-in, cherry phosphates at Carney's Drug Store, and double features at the Diana.

However, by 1965, Tipton's enchanted, insulated days of blind bliss were headed for an iniquitous dissolution. No one saw it coming, but when it blew into town, it could not be swept away.

It began October 16, the night Olene Emberton didn't come home. Last seen alive shortly before midnight, she was found a day and half later, her lifeless body discarded alongside a country lane five and a half miles northeast of the Tipton city limits. For those who knew and loved Olene, her death was a defining marker in their lives.

Nothing quite like it had happened in the town's one-hundred-twenty-year history. People were scared, confused, and suspicious. They sensed something sacred had been lost. Their innocence and their perceived place in the world had been betrayed; but worse, one of their precious children had been snatched from them. Front doors that previously were never locked became routinely bolted. Parents, who had not worried when their children were out of their sight, now kept them on a short rein. Although strangers had always evoked a furtive sizing up as they passed through, after Olene's death, they were studied with suspicion.

With no cause of death, no clues, no witnesses, no leads, and nowhere to go, Olene Emberton's story bears the hallmarks of a legend. Yet, let's never forget that long before she was a legend, she was an ordinary girl with hopes and dreams for a bright future.

Growing up in the 1950s and '60s, we Tipton kids generally knew one another well — who lived where, how we spent our time, who went with who, each other's likes and dislikes, and their plans beyond high school. Olene, however, was one of those kids who were hard to read, unless you happened to be one of her close friends. She tended to stick with her own small group, to project a standoffish air. We had been classmates since fourth grade. We were both members of the Tipton High School Class of '66 and shared scores of school happenings. We lived *two blocks* apart. We should have bonded. But like so many others in our class, I didn't really know her. Beyond her quiet, well-mannered exterior, I had no clue of what hopes and dreams dwelled in her heart, or what joys and fears fueled her emotions.

Looking back now, through the lens of an adult entering her

eighth decade of life experience, I realize I didn't know Olene well because we had so little in common. She was reserved, while I was gregarious. She was mature, while I was childish. She was studious, while I merely got by. She went to church regularly. I rarely did. Her parents kept a tight leash on her. My parents' leash had some give. Olene and I moved in different circles and followed different paths. My path was unencumbered; hers was destined for a dead end.

The notion of writing about her first occurred to me some thirty years ago. I was living in Southern California and had come home to Tipton to visit my parents for a few days. One afternoon, I ran into a couple of old classmates, and we began talking about Olene. I was surprised to learn that two decades had not tempered conventional wisdom about her tragic death. The rumors were astonishing. The misinformation was as ludicrous and unfair as ever, and it bothered me. Olene did not deserve the sullied annotation about her character and her terrible ending. Someone needed to set the record straight. Could it be me?

Perhaps, I thought, but not yet. I still lacked the skills and know-how to undertake a project of that magnitude. But by the mid-2000s, I had been a staff writer at *The Times* in Frankfort, Indiana, for five years. I had honed the research and reporting skills that such an undertaking would require and developed a basic comprehension of criminal investigation. That's when I got serious about acting on my long-held desire to honor and remember my classmate by telling her story. I dug through court records and news articles, interviewed law enforcement officials who had helped work the case, sent Freedom of Information Act requests, talked with Olene's friends and classmates, tracked down loose ends, and attempted to snap the puzzle pieces together.

In 2007, after giving Olene's story two years of investigative diligence, I hit a speed bump. I asked for her family's blessing to write the book, and they weren't ready to give it. At that point, I set all my work aside, uncertain whether I would ever pick it up again.

Fast-forward nine years. In early 2016, two opportunities

emerged to get the project moving again: First, I got the nod from Olene's only remaining, immediate family member in Tipton — her sister-in-law, Debbie Emberton; and second, I met Nicole Kobrowski, an amazing, Westfield-based author with several Indiana folklore books to her credit and an affinity for true crime.

When I told Nicole about Olene and showed her my volumes of research, she felt an instant kinship. She urged me to finish the book, and I recognized a golden opportunity. I invited her to team up with me, and without hesitation, she promised to be my cheerleader, advisor, and editor.

I owe so much to Debbie and Nicole. Without them, my notes would still be in a binder stashed in the closet, and I would still be filled with anxiety, worrying whether I should write the book.

METHODOLOGY

The interviews I conducted in the mid 2000s with officials and others who had first-hand knowledge of the case were as informative as they were generous. I'm forever grateful to those individuals for speaking with me on the record, but they were only the beginning. I needed additional sources, and as I sought them, I stumbled over two major challenges: time and attrition. Many key officials, Emberton family members, and friends had passed away or could not be located. Still others could no longer remember. In an effort to combat the memory issue, I conducted two group interviews composed of Olene's classmates. The sessions were enjoyable, high-energy events that encouraged the attendees to talk freely and share memories, which sparked new recollections and clarified questionable ones.

Not everyone who wanted to submit their Olene memories for the book was able to attend one of the get-togethers. So, I sent them a questionnaire or conducted a phone interview. Response was gratifying, and I am confident that everyone who wanted to contribute was able to do so.

It's important to note that not everyone I wanted to inter-

Pictured is Mrs. Lacy's 1959 fifth-grade class at Jefferson Elementary. The girl in the circle at the top is me. The other girl circled is Olene.

view for the book was willing without a caveat. For example, a few declined to talk to me at all, while some agreed to talk "off the record" — meaning I could use the information they provided as long as I kept my word not to identify them as the source.

In addition to gathering first-person accounts, I searched for public records that might add to my understanding of Olene's case. For example, in the absence of official case files from the Tipton Police and the Tipton County Sheriff's Department, I filed a Freedom of Information Act request with the Indiana State Police. When it was declined, I scoured newspaper reports and court documents for clues — bits of new information, off-handed remarks, conclusions that didn't add up, inconsistencies, and errors. The *Tipton Tribune, Kokomo Tribune, Indianapolis Star,* and papers from many other Indiana cities covered the Emberton case for weeks. I organized their original reports in sequential order. The result was a timeline of the manner in which the investigation unfolded, a compilation of on-the-record facts about the case, and a greater understanding of how it had been communicated to the public.

Thus, utilizing my newspaper reporting skills, I presented the bulk of Olene's story as a typical, nonfiction, true crime narrative. Yet much of her story is also an oral history, thanks to Olene's classmates, friends, and relatives who generously shared their memories about her and the events related to the case. In addition, because of my long-time involvement with this project and having been a member of Olene's class, I was compelled to occasionally insert myself into the storytelling with my own memories, insight, and reporting experience from a first-person perspective. The five chapters written from my personal perspective are identified with the phrase, "Author's Point of View," preceding the chapter title.

I want to stress that, as can be expected in a project of this nature, my research sometimes led me down dark paths that involved other people's tragedies and pain. Thus, in every instance where including names would have proved hurtful or in some way detrimental to a particular person or their family, I approached the subject with sensitivity and, whenever possible, refrained from identifying individuals to protect and respect their privacy.

The pages that follow recount, as best as I understand it, a significant, tragic episode of Tipton's past that stole a young woman's life, cheated the world of the promise of her contributions, and tore her family apart. My great hope for this book is its acceptance alongside the Tipton community's historic records for future generations to read, absorb, and share. To do so, in a sense, will keep Olene Emberton alive.

AND FINALLY

I also studied the aforementioned rumors, which tainted the truth and helped create the legend. I picked them apart, looking for even the thinnest shred of possibility. When none could be found, I dismissed them all and turned to informed logic.

Was I able to come up with a conclusive answer to how Olene died? Sadly, I wasn't. I still don't know equivocally whether her death was the deliberate act of a murderer, if it was an unexpected natural occurrence, or if it was the accidental consequence of a careless aggressor who then panicked and abandoned her body next to that cornfield. (Incidentally, per Indiana Code §23-14-54, it is a Class B misdemeanor in Indiana to dispose of a body in this manner.)

I simply don't know the answer. But there is one thing I do know with unshakable certainty: Whoever watched Olene die, and then, with callous disregard for human decency, discarded her body alongside that road should not have enjoyed a moment's peace since.

In my opinion, only one person within Olene's scope fits the profile of a dangerous predator devoid of a conscience and respect for life. Of course, that distinction taken by itself does not equate to guilt. In the absence of physical evidence, a witness, or a confession, my opinion is just that — my opinion.

Thus, for my purposes, I decided early on that drawing conclusions would not be the point of this book. Rather, I viewed this book as the vehicle for procuring and assembling Olene's story as objectively, truthfully, respectfully, and as complete and detailed as I could.

Once that was accomplished, the final step was turning it over to readers so they could arrive at their own conclusions and their own verdicts. Thus, it's in your hands now.

Murder or misdemeanor?

You decide.

Janis Thornton
June 30, 2018

The front page of the Saturday, October 16, 1965, Tipton Tribune *is dominated by the wrapup of Friday's homecoming parade and football game, which gave Tipton a satisfying victory over Alexandria, 32-21. The next edition of the local paper would carry a story announcing the disappearance of Olene Emberton, although her body would have been found just two hours before the paper started hitting doorsteps. (Reprint of cover courtesy the* Tipton Tribune.*)*

1

AUTHOR'S POINT OF VIEW:
THE DAY SOMETHING INIQUITOUS BLEW INTO TOWN

I will always remember Saturday, October 16, 1965. I had been looking forward to that date for weeks. I had it circled on my calendar. In red. It was supposed to be a fun-filled day of happiness and celebration.

My boyfriend, who was a year ahead of me in school, came home that weekend for the first time since moving to Bloomington for his freshman year at Indiana University. It was homecoming weekend. We went to dinner that evening with my just-married friends, who had recently settled into their first home together and were already expecting their first child. We had a lot to feel joyful about.

Unfortunately, it turned out to be anything but joyful. Instead, for me and scores of others, October 16, 1965, became synonymous with profound tragedy and despair. It was the night Olene Emberton didn't come home.

Back then, round-the-clock news was unheard of and Tipton did not have a Sunday newspaper. That's why most of Tipton remained blissfully ignorant about Olene's disappearance until Monday's *Tipton Tribune* hit the doorsteps around 4:00 p.m. Twenty more hours would pass before Tuesday's edition would go to press carrying the headline story of Olene's death.

I, on the other hand, as a high school student, had access to a fast-moving news network comprised of classmates. Through this grapevine, I became aware Monday morning at the start of my second-period class that Olene was unaccounted for, and I learned of her death before I returned home from school some eight hours later.

At just past nine o'clock Monday morning, I was seated with my best friend, Gail Perdue (now Wix), at one of the round tables in the home economics classroom waiting for Louise McIntosh's Family Living class to start. As the other students strolled in, I overheard someone say that Olene was missing. Gail and I immediately looked at each other and smirked. No love was lost between Gail and Olene. Both girls had spent months competing for the same boy, and my loyalty would always be Gail's. So, when it came to whatever Olene was up to, we shrugged it off.

Maybe she had run away to get married, Gail said, hopefully. Although it wasn't an everyday occurrence, teenagers occasionally ran off together and eloped. So, we thought if that were the case with Olene, we didn't envy her for the punishment her parents would undoubtely impose once she was back home. And the fact is, a parent's wrath was the worst consequence I could imagine. The possibility that she was in any sort of danger never entered my mind. At that point in my life, the notion that anyone living in Tipton, Indiana, could be in mortal danger was inconceivable.

However, my sense of security started to unravel that afternoon, when our principal, Charles Edwards, delayed school dismissal and called several students to his office. What remained of my tattered perception of invulnerability completely disintegrated about an hour later as Gail and I kicked back in my '52 Plymouth at Jim Dandy Drive-in sipping root beer and speculating on Olene. Gail had been one of the students called to the office, so, by then, we suspected that whatever happened to Olene had nothing to do with a secret elopement.

Young-Nichols Funeral Home was located across the street from the drive-in. Our curiosity was piqued when we observed one of the Young-Nichols white ambulances cruise past us and pull into the alley just west of the mortuary.

Where had it been? Who had it picked up? Olene? Had it transported her to the Tipton hospital?

Our classmate John O'Banion, who had been parked in the spot next to us, also had seen the Young-Nichols vehicle. Because he was a close friend of Olene's brother Floyd Wayne, I was certain John was asking himself the same questions. He climbed out of his car without hesitation and hurried across the street. A few minutes later, he returned, his face stern and bearing an odd, pained expression.

I asked if he'd found out whether the ambulance's run had anything to do with Olene. His answer was not at all what I expected or wanted to hear.

"Yes," he said, "she's dead."

John obviously was deeply affected by the development, and considering his close relationship with the family, I marvel today at his steady composure as he articulated the unthinkable.

Over the years, looking back through the fog of time, as hard as I've tried to recall my reaction to John's simple but devastating statement, "Yes, she's dead," my memory is a blank. I have no recollection whatsoever of my words or my feelings in that moment. In retrospect, I don't think I knew how or what to feel. It took many years before the meaning of Olene's death completely registered with me. I was in my thirties before I could fully comprehend how her mysterious, untimely passing had penetrated what I perceived then as an invisible wall protecting my hometown from outside evil forces; but most importantly, to grasp how unanswered questions surrounding her death broke the hearts and spirits of everyone who loved her, her family most of all.

I have never understood why it took me so long to process the full gravity of this tragic loss, and I regret that it did. Perhaps that regret is what fuels my passion to preserve Olene's memory by telling her story. •

> *"What you've been looking for*
> *has been found."*
> — Tipton County Dispatcher

2
LOST AND FOUND

The search for Olene Emberton had been underway for twenty-six hours when, shortly past 2:00 p.m. Monday, October 18, the Tipton County dispatcher answered an emergency call, originating from a farmhouse north of Hobbs. The male caller reported an unresponsive woman lying alongside a desolate country lane in the northeastern part of the county. The dispatcher immediately radioed a cryptic bulletin to the sheriff: "What you've been looking for has been found."

An account of what happened next was described by Jim Pratt during an interview conducted at his home in October 2006. Pratt served as Tipton Police Chief from 1962 to 1972 and had first-hand knowledge of the events that transpired the afternoon Olene's body was found.

He and Tipton County Sheriff Verl Grimme had met on the east side of Green Street, two doors north of its intersection with North Street, to dust Olene's red, 1957 Chevrolet for fingerprints. Indiana State Trooper Michael Colgate, Tipton County Prosecutor Richard Regnier, and Olene's parents, Floyd and Roxie Emberton, had joined them. Olene's car had been parked in that location on Green Street, a mere three-and-a-half blocks from the Embertons' Sweetland Avenue home, since around midnight Saturday, according to one of the neighbors.

When Pratt heard the dispatcher's message waft through the radio in the sheriff's cruiser, he peered across the roof of the red Chevy and locked eyes with Grimme.

A stone-faced Grimme flashed a look at Pratt, strolled back to his brown and tan cruiser, climbed in behind the wheel, and started the motor. The Embertons either hadn't heard the dispatcher's message or were unaware of its significance and, without question, accepted the sheriff's apology for his sudden departure.

Speeding away, Grimme radioed the dispatcher for directions and details. The dispatcher told him that the caller had not said whether the victim was alive or dead, only that she appeared to have been raped. Grimme felt certain the victim was Olene, but he wouldn't know until he saw her that she was dead. After confirming that the Young-Nichols ambulance had been called, Grimme instructed the dispatcher to tell its driver *not* to use the siren. A bunch of curiosity seekers getting in the way at the scene was the last thing he needed.

Grimme mashed his gas pedal to the floor and headed north up State Road 19 to Division Road, where he made a right turn on two squealing tires. When he'd traveled four-and-a-half miles, he spun the car to the left, down a narrow, gravel lane that was nearly obscured by the fields of corn flanking it. About a half mile up, he spotted Larry Clouser, the farmer whose mother had found Olene.

Clouser gestured to a spot on the east side of the road. He would later tell the *Tipton Tribune* that his mother had discovered the body when she began to open the gate to the soybean field he was preparing to harvest. He said his mother had been so badly shaken, she was nearly unable to form the words to tell him what she had seen.

Grimme pulled his car up to Clouser, shifted into Park, and climbed out. Clouser directed Grimme's attention to the victim's body lying in the ankle-high grass between the road and the wire fence lining the field. The instant Grimme saw Olene, he likely realized that his hopes for her had been too lofty. •

"That's the last time I saw her…"
— Mollie Russell

3
SATURDAY: DAWN TO DOOM

Forty-eight hours earlier, Olene had been a giddy seventeen-year-old, practically dancing on air as she rushed about, getting herself ready for the wedding of her dear friends, Mollie Reecer and Mike Russell. They were getting married that afternoon at Church of Christ, the Emberton family's church, located on the northeast corner of Jefferson Street and Sweetland Avenue.

"Olene had been happy all day as she worked around the house," her mother, Roxie Emberton, said as reported in a December 3, 1965, *Kokomo Tribune* story. "She was happy and normal in every way that last day."

According to Roxie, she and her only daughter had always enjoyed a close relationship. Olene often talked about her future, which included college the following year at Ball State University in preparation for a teaching career.

Olene also hoped for a wedding of her own some day.

"We had talked about a church wedding Saturday morning," Roxie told the *Kokomo Tribune*, "and Olene told me the name of the boy she wanted to marry. … As it came time to go, Olene told me, 'Hurry, Mother, hurry.' She was excited and wanted to sit near the front so she could see the bride's gown."

The *Indianapolis Star* reported that Olene had caught the

Girl Missing From Home

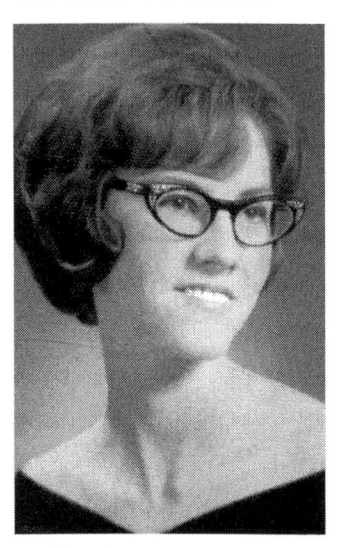

Miss Olene Emberton, 17, a junior at Tipton High School and daughter of Mr. and Mrs. Floyd Emberton, 335 Sweetland, Tipton, has been reported missing by her parents, since 11:30 p.m. Saturday. Tipton County Sheriff Verl Grimme is conducting a search for her and said she was last known to be in the community when, after taking a date home in her family car, she parked and locked the machine at North and Green Streets at approximately 11:30.

The missing girl is slender, blue eyed with brown hair, standing 5'4" and weighing 104 pounds. When last seen she was wearing a white blouse and charcoal grey skirt, a maroon sweater and was carrying a black purse. Anyone to have seen her after 11:30 Saturday night is asked to contact the family or authorities.

A story announcing that Olene Emberton had been missing since late Saturday night appeared on the front page of the Monday, October 18, 1965, Tipton Tribune. The story was out of date even before it hit the first doorstep Monday afternoon. (Reproduction of the Tipton Tribune article.)

bride's bouquet thrown after the ceremony.

More than fifty years after her wedding, Mollie Russell says she still thinks of Olene "every single day."

It's impossible to know whether Olene's disappearance later that day might have been averted if ordinary events that preceded the tragedy had lined up differently.

During an April 2017 interview, Russell explained that because Mike had been in the Army, based at Fort Knox, Kentucky, until a few hours before the wedding, they were uncertain whether their wedding plans could be played out.

"That week, we weren't even sure we were going to get married because we weren't sure Mike could get there," she said.

And that wasn't the only reason for their uncertainty. They had failed to meet the state's required three-day wait between the day their marriage license was granted and the day of the wedding.

"We needed special permission from the judge to get married," she continued, "and Mike's parents had to sign for him because he was under age."

In light of the tragedy that happened on her wedding day, Russell had been haunted for decades with a question that no one can ever answer.

"I think maybe if I'd had [Olene] be the third bride's maid maybe she ..."

Russell let her regret linger unspoken for a moment. Then she recalled her last memory of her dear friend.

"When we were leaving the church," she said, her eyes growing moist, "I looked back, and Olene was standing at the top of the stairs." She paused to choke back a sudden surge of emotion. A beat passed. Her composure restored, she continued her story. "That's the last time I saw her ... the last thing I remember."

Olene dropped off her gift for the newlyweds during their wedding reception at Tipton's popular Tom's Cafeteria, located at the downtown intersection of Jefferson and Independence Streets, but Russell had no recollection of the gift or of seeing Olene there.

Olene hadn't stayed long. She was eager to return home to prepare for her movie date that evening with classmate Phil Roudebush. According to an October 20, 1965, *Indianapolis News* story, the date would be her second with Roudebush; and, according to a November 30 *Kokomo Tribune* article, her first date with anyone since July.

"I think it was the second time we'd gone out," Roudebush explained during an April 2018 interview. "Olene and I weren't strangers. We met riding the school bus in sixth grade, and we went on hayrides. I went to Lutheran School, and she went to Jefferson [Elementary School] and then junior high. So we kind of lost touch until high school. So, we were not socializing a lot. We moved in different worlds.

"When we got to high school, I was seeing somebody, and she was seeing somebody," he continued, "but when that senior year came around, we had stopped seeing those people, so we went out a couple times."

Both had looked forward to their date that night. As soon as Olene arrived home from the wedding reception, she changed from the pretty dress she'd worn to the wedding into a crisp white blouse, a charcoal-grey skirt, and her maroon sweater. She wore a gold necklace and tucked a neatly folded Kleenex and her red billfold into her black clutch purse.

She was all ready to go when Roudebush arrived to pick her up. But, as Roudebush explained, "My car was down … a transmission problem … so I walked down to her house, and we were going to walk to the movie."

The Diana Theatre was a block east of the courthouse square, ten blocks from Olene's house, and as Roudebush recalled, the night was chilly.

But Olene had an idea.

"Olene asked her date if it was all right for her to drive,"

Roxie noted in her December 7, 1965, *Kokomo Tribune* interview. Roudebush didn't mind. So they climbed into her car and drove off. "That was the last time I was to see her," Roxie said.

The double feature playing at the Diana was an Edgar Allen Poe adaptation called "Tomb of Ligeia," starring Hollywood's master of horror films, Vincent Price, and a less exciting film titled "Operation Snafu," starring a very young and little-known Sean Connery. Admission for the couple, plus popcorn and soft drinks, set Roudebush back about $4.50, a hefty amount for a high school student in 1965. The lights dimmed at seven o'clock. The combined running time of the movies was approximately three hours. Add to that the

This ad appeared on page six of the Tipton Tribune *on Wednesday, October 13, 1965, promoting* Tomb of Ligeia *and* Operation Snafu, *the double feature which played at Tipton's Diana Theatre from that Wednesday through Saturday, October 16. The ad lists the starting times for* Tomb of Ligeia *as 7:00 and 10:05 p.m. (Reprint courtesy the* Tipton Tribune.)

time required for the cartoon and trailers, and it can be surmised that the couple would have departed the theater by shortly past 10:00 p.m., although the October 19 *Tipton Tribune* reported that they had left around 11:00 p.m. From there, it is known that they drove to Six Acres, a popular drive-in restaurant at the east edge of town on State Road 28.

In those days, Six Acres was *the* place for teenagers to be seen, to see who was with whom, catch up on news and gossip, and maybe even stop for a burger. Most, however, simply cruised the parking lot, turning onto the lot at the entrance just west of the drive-in and making one pass around the building — with their car radio blaring, their passengers waving and shouting, honking the horn, and some of the more daring passengers hanging halfway out a window — and out the exit back onto the highway. Many of the drivers cruised the horseshoe-shaped route repeatedly — in and out, around and around.

According to Roudebush, as quoted in the October 19, 1965, edition of the *Tipton Tribune*, he and Olene cruised around Six Acres one time, didn't stop, and headed back into town. During Roxie's December 7 interview with the *Kokomo Tribune*, she said the teens had noticed Olene's 16-year-old brother, Floyd Wayne, walking west on Jefferson Street. Olene stopped to pick him up and dropped him off at the Embertons'.

In the same *Kokomo Tribune* interview, Roxie stated that she heard someone come home at 10:20 that night and thought it was her daughter. She wouldn't realize until the next morning that it had been Floyd Wayne.

"Olene had brought him home and then left to take her date home," Roxie said.

Assuming Roxie's timing was accurate, it's remarkable to consider that just a little more than an hour before Olene was last seen alive, she had been so close to the safety of home. And, once again, it should be noted that the tragedy awaiting her might never have occurred if that night's events had been acted out in a slightly different order; i.e., had she dropped off Roudebush first and then driven straight home with her brother beside her riding shotgun.

After Floyd Wayne was out of the car, Olene headed for the Roudebush home at the intersection of Main and North Streets.

"She insisted that she drop me off so I didn't have to walk," Roudebush said.

After they arrived at his house, the two teenagers sat in the car and chatted for a few more minutes.

According to the October 19 *Tipton Tribune*, at around 11:30 p.m., Olene admitted that she was tired. She'd had a full day and was eager to crawl into her bed. So the two said their good-byes, Roudebush climbed out of the car, and Olene sped off, headed west, bound for home.

"And that's the moment I have to live with," he said. "Who'd have ever thought…? It was just six blocks from my house to hers."•

4
AUTHOR'S POINT OF VIEW: ANALYSES OF THE CRIME SCENE

The moment Mrs. Clouser discovered Olene's body, she and her son, Larry, rushed back to the house and phoned the county dispatcher. Because Mrs. Clouser had become so emotionally distraught by what she'd seen, it is reasonable to assume her son was the one who made the call. He, too, was emotionally charged, and somehow, somewhere between him and Sheriff Grimme, a miscommunication occurred. Either Clouser had been unaware that Olene was dead, or the dispatcher had misunderstood what Clouser told her, or perhaps Grimme had misinterpreted the dispatcher. Regardless of who was at fault, once the sheriff processed the message, he told the dispatcher to have Phil Nichols, owner of Young-Nichols Funeral Home and one of the two local ambulance services, to drive his ambulance to the crime scene. Nichols wouldn't know until he got there that the emergency involved a death.

In the early spring of 2006, Phil Nichols afforded me forty-five minutes for an interview at his office in the funeral home, which had served the Tipton community for decades. While Nichols had been in the family business all his life, he also had served as Tipton County coroner for five terms, his first being 1961-1964.

I asked him if he had thought he'd been summoned to a death

scene when he received the dispatcher's call the afternoon of Monday, October 18, 1965.

"No," he said.

I asked him to describe what he had seen.

"I still remember it," he said. "She was lying in the side ditch. Her clothes were all stacked up very neatly beside her. ... She was on her back, east to west. Her head was toward the east. I don't think she died right there. I think she was placed there."

Had he seen any man-made marks, I asked, such as scratches and bruises?

He hadn't noticed any, he said.

Did he remember seeing insect bites on her body?

"Several," he said.

I asked if he recalled law enforcement officials at the scene other than the sheriff.

"Yes," he said, "deputies and state police. The city police wouldn't have been out there."

I expressed concern that the crime scene might have been unintentionally contaminated, and Nichols remarked that the officers would have known better than to disturb potential evidence.

As the interview was wrapping up, Nichols suggested I speak with Robert Zell, a former Indiana State Police officer who had been involved in the investigation from the first day.

I met with Bob Zell in June of 2006 at his home in Tipton, located just three blocks up the street from where I lived.

Zell, then 81, was gracious and welcoming. His service to the state police had extended from 1948 through January 1969, when he retired having attained the rank of sergeant. After a few minutes of polite small talk, I turned our conversation to the reason for my visit — Olene Emberton, whose death he helped investigate four decades before.

He immediately told me, almost apologetically, "I hadn't thought about that case in years until you called. I don't know how much help I can be. My memory is very vague on that whole situation."

I assured him I had confidence in his memory and began the interview with a question about the manner in which he had been called into the case.

"The body was still there when I got there," Zell said without hesitation. "So I'm assuming Verl radioed Pendleton for assistance, and I was the handiest one, so I got sent. I was out there before the coroner had even picked up the body and taken it away."

I asked him to describe what he saw when he arrived at the scene. He said:

Looking north, this is the desolate, northeast Tipton County road — North 450 East as it appears today — where Olene's body was found the afternoon of Monday, October 18, 1965. The "X" indicates the approximate location where she had lain.

"It was just an open farm field. There were no houses around, so nobody was there. I saw her lying there in the ditch alongside the road. It's a gravel road, and there was a drainage ditch. ... She was lying on her back at an angle to the road, and her head was up near the fence. She was well back off the road. There was no possibility that someone was going to accidentally run over her. She was well over in the grass and completely nude.

"There were no marks that I can recall. She was bleeding slightly from the vagina. ... As I recall, there were no marks like strangulation, or hand marks or bruises or anything, and certainly no open injuries of any kind on the body."

Zell said he was nearby as the investigators conducted their search of the crime scene. He recalled observing the officers as they wandered the grounds, sifting through the grass looking for evidence, and he was confident they were following standard protocol. I asked him if, in his opinion, the investigation of the crime scene was conducted as professionally as possible. He believed it had been, he said, and then explained:

"I think it was for the level of knowledge and training that they had at that time. Not pertaining to this case, but I remember on various situations where we would get calls to investigate something — like a small town police department would call for help, and it was a serious problem sometimes, or a sheriff and deputies would go to a crime scene and walk all around the place and pick stuff up and lay it down and move around, and by the time any of our people would get there, it's no longer an original crime scene. They would have contaminated everything.

"With [the Emberton case], I don't know that anything like that happened because there weren't that many people involved in it initially, and it was out away from where local people could mingle and walk around. Those kinds of things did happen, but not so much anymore because they've all had training in how to secure crime scenes.

"At that time, the sheriff one day is driving a truck, or whatever, and he gets elected. They put a uniform and badge on him, and he's the sheriff."

I considered what he'd told me and said, "I assume you and all the other officers there that day looked for any kind of clue that might help explain what had happened."

To that, he said, "Yeah, I couldn't even tell you now whether we found anything."

According to all the other sources I spoke with, they didn't, and without physical evidence, investigators' best hope for solving the case rested with the autopsy and witness testimony. Unfortunately, neither was what they hoped for.

* * *

Marshall "Marty" Talbert served as an Indiana State Police officer from 1977 through 2002. He retired from the I.S.P. in 2003 after he was elected Howard County Sheriff. He served two terms.

In 1993, while assigned to the state police investigation of the 1990 murder of a nineteen-year-old woman in Valparaiso, he discovered what he thought could be a link to the unsolved Emberton case. He revisited all the leads the state and Tipton County investigators pursued in 1965 but was never able to conclusively prove his hunch.

Now semi-retired but still projecting the air of a no-nonsense, dedicated law man, Talbert talked with me on a Saturday morning in February 2018 at Faye's Northside Café. I was grateful that throughout our two-hour chat, he reined in his naturally intimidating demeanor, a handy attribute when dealing with hardened criminals, and instead projected his congenial, good-natured side. Chugging down cups of coffee, he answered my many questions about Olene's case in animated detail. At my request, he also explained several of the differences between criminal investigation practices of 1965 and those of today.

Talbert said he had been enjoying breakfast and lunch at Faye's Northside Café since the early 1990s, when he was seeking information about the Emberton case. Back then, he often sat with Tipton people, many of whom readily discussed the case with him. Among them was Larry Clouser, who related to Talbert the startling details of finding Olene's body discarded on his property.

"Larry took me out there and showed me the spot," Talbert recalled. "It was just a field access road. He said he frequently saw policemen walking the fields in the spring after the crime occurred. He was adamant that he had seen a white car driving up and down that roadway for months, but he could never get a license plate for it."

One aspect of Olene's case that always bothered Talbert was not knowing why she left her car at the intersection of Green and North Streets.

"Olene's car was found in that neighborhood, where it was deposited," he said, "and we don't know whether she was abducted or went willingly. You would have thought that when she left the car there, if she was uncomfortable with the situation, she would have screamed. Obviously, if she parked and left it there, she wasn't in distress."

He continued, "When you're on late-night patrol, if you find a car in a shopping center or a cemetery, you would contact the owner because the car seems out of place. But if it's parked in a residential neighborhood, it doesn't attract attention. It doesn't seem out of place."

Another aspect of Olene's case that always bothered Talbert was the medical examiner's inability to determine cause of death.

"There was a question of whether [Olene's death] was a homicide or an accident," he said. "There wasn't a history of missing girls in Tipton County, and I think the total lack of clues and physical evidence pretty much stymied the investigation."

Perhaps all the unanswered questions could have been satisfied if the necessary technology and science had been developed and available to the investigators.

"Back then," Talbert said, "forensic science wasn't nearly as advanced. DNA testing, for example, hadn't been developed. A lot of the evidence was based on witness statements, but today, there are so many more things we can do, like looking at social media accounts, cell phones, and email."

These days, when bodies are discovered, Talbert said, the lead investigator calls the crime scene tech to the site. If the corpse was found outside and had been exposed to the elements, the tech would perform tests based on numerous soil samples taken from under the body. The tech would also wrap the hands and take nail scrapings, the clothes would be packaged, and DNA would be analyzed.

"An interesting question would be, how much homicide experience did the sheriff have," Talbert said, "and how much death scene experience? Did Tipton County even *have* a death scene investigator?"

Talbert added that, based on the accounts he read concerning Olene's case, and from information gathered from people he talked with, such as Richard Regnier, who had been the Tipton County prosecutor at that time, her death did not appear to be a murder.

"There were no wounds on her body," Talbert said, "and it didn't have the characteristics of being a homicide. The autopsy results were inconclusive as to exact cause of death, and even if you could have tied somebody to this, you don't know if criminal charges would have been warranted."

In conclusion, Talbert said, "Olene's car being parked in that neighborhood and nobody hearing anything or seeing anything seems to indicate that she went willingly with someone she knew." •

These photos show the intersection of Green and North Streets as it appears today. The top picture looks west on North Street, the bottom looks north on Green. The white vehicle in the lower photo is positioned in the approximate spot where Olene parked her car the night she went missing.

> *"You'll find her dead
> in some ditch somewhere."*
> — Floyd Emberton

5
HOPE TO HEARTACHE

"I knew when I discovered Sunday morning that she had not been home all night that something terrible had happened," Roxie Emberton told the *Kokomo Tribune* for its Olene Emberton update on December 7, 1965. "I started screaming as soon as I looked in her bedroom and saw her bed had not been slept in."

Floyd phoned the sheriff's office at 10:00 a.m. to report Olene missing. He then went out looking for her and found her car parked in the 400 block of Green Street, headed north. Perhaps it was the sight of the abandoned automobile that sparked Floyd's ominous premonition.

When Tipton Chief of Police Jim Pratt went to the Emberton home to take the missing person report, Floyd told him, "You'll find her dead in some ditch somewhere." The Embertons did not elaborate, Pratt said.

Although, forty-eight days later, Roxie would tell the *Kokomo Tribune* that Olene never stayed away unexpectedly. "She always called me and let me know if she was going to be late. That's why I knew when I discovered she was not home Sunday morning that something terrible had happened."

The last person known to have seen Olene, Phil Roudebush, recounted the painful moment he learned of her disappearance.

"The phone is ringing, and Mom comes up to see if I'm there," Roudebush said. "It was the Embertons saying Olene wasn't home. I immediately jumped in the car and headed that way. I pulled up to the flashing light at Green Street and saw her car there, parked perfectly straight, locked. I checked the car to make sure nobody was there and went on to her mom and dad's."

The family customarily attended Sunday worship services at Tipton Church of Christ. It was a small congregation, and all the families were close, according to Olene's friend and classmate, Patricia Brooks. She also had attended the Reecer-Russell wedding the afternoon before and knew about Olene's plans to attend the movie that evening. Church the next morning was where Brooks first heard of Olene's disappearance.

"Everyone was talking about it," Brooks wrote in a 2017 email. "No one had seen or heard from Olene since she dropped Phil off at home after the movie. We stopped by the Embertons' home after church to see if they had heard anything from her. They were extremely worried and upset."

After the service, others from the Church of Christ congregation gathered around the Embertons at their home to pray for them and show support. Police questioned twenty or more of Olene's friends in hopes of uncovering a lead, and murmurs of Olene's disappearance were soon rippling through the greater Tipton community.

The parents of Mollie Reecer and Mike Russell received a call Sunday morning from Sheriff Grimme.

"He was wanting to know where we went," Mollie Russell said during her April 2017 interview. "He was trying to find us. He wanted to know if Olene might have gone with us. But nobody knew where we were because *we* didn't know where we were going. We only had so much time before Mike had to get back to Fort Knox."

* * *

Students arriving at Tipton High School Monday morning were still fired up by the varsity football team's 32-21 win Friday night over Alexandria. The Blue Devils' conquest helped the team atone for an embarrassing losing season, while giving the students, visiting alumni, and fans a satisfying homecoming victory.

Pouring into the halls, the kids noisily greeted one another as they hustled to outrun the bell for first-period classes. That was where most of them heard about Olene.

Tom Preston, who dated Olene for several months until they broke up the previous July, was among the few students already aware of the situation when they arrived at school on Monday. Although there is no record of a conversation the previous day between Preston and Olene's father, it's likely Floyd would have phoned Preston seeking clues to Olene's whereabouts.

According to the October 19 *Tipton Tribune*, Sheriff Grimme contacted Preston Sunday afternoon, encouraging him to stop by the jail, along with several other youths, for questioning. As it turned out, Preston spent the night in jail with Phil Roudebush. Both boys were held for their own protection as a precaution because of Floyd's unpredictable temper, although both Preston and Roudebush were allowed to attend school.

Ed Achenbach, who had been one of Preston's closest confidant's, revealed during a December 2016 interview that Preston had been quite upset that Monday morning after Olene went missing. Preston had been so emotionally rattled that as soon as he entered the school building, he made a dash for the second-floor boys' restroom to try to calm down with a smoke. A moment later, Achenbach unwittingly walked in on his good friend and was stunned by what he saw.

"Tom was pale and visibly shaking," Achenbach said. "He told me about Olene and said he'd spent the night in protective custody at the jail."

Stunned and confused, Achenbach sputtered, "Why?"

Preston explained that he had received threats on Sunday from Floyd Emberton, and the only way the sheriff could ensure everyone's safety was by locking Preston up — in essence, locking Emberton out.

As the news about Olene spread from student to student, some dismissed their teachers' worry and speculated with awe that she had run away, perhaps to meet a boy. Tipton High School students were inexperienced in the evils of the world. If a cavalier attitude regarding Olene's wellbeing existed, it should be attributed more to a lack of experience and imagination than to a lack of caring. Even as the morning faded into afternoon with no news of her whereabouts, many felt Olene had merely pulled a stunt. No one doubted she would eventually turn up safe and sound.

On normal school days, the last bell sounded at 3:20 p.m. to signal the dismissal of school. That day, however, at about three o'clock, the P.A. system crackled and the voice of Principal Charles Edwards announced that the dismissal would be delayed. Although it was unprecedented, he told students to stay put at their desks until further notice, except for approximately twenty students, whose names he proceeded to read off.

Most of the high school students, and virtually *all* the members of the senior class, were aware Olene had been missing since Saturday night, but until that announcement from Edwards, few, if any, of the students comprehended the gravity of what was happening. Certainly, even then, no one expected what was coming.

After Edwards had recited the last of the students' names, he said they all were to report to the school office ... *"Now!"*

In a January 2017 letter, Gail Wix shared her recollection of the circumstances and events surrounding Olene's disappearance and death. She wrote:

> "I remember [Mr. Edwards] reading off a list of names. I was one of those names. I was scared to death.

I had never been called to the office before.

"In the office, there was Mr. Edwards, our guidance counselor, Mrs. [Patricia] Moore, and Sheriff Grimme. I had no idea why I was there, but as the questions were asked of me, I understood.

"Sheriff Grimme asked where I had been Saturday night, who I had been with, and what we did. I answered all his questions. ... He asked if I knew Olene's car had been found parked about a block away from where I lived. I was shocked to hear that. I told him 'No.' He asked questions until I thought I was in real trouble. When I thought it couldn't get any worse, he asked me if I had stabbed Olene with a knife. I was horrified! I told him the entire story, which took all of two minutes.

"I had been working at Carney's [Drug Store, where Olene also worked] behind the soda counter making someone a banana split, so I had the knife in my hand to cut the banana in half. Olene was in front of me, while I was talking to someone else. When she stopped, I ran into her and the knife nicked her arm. It was a stupid accident that I was very sorry for. It barely brought blood, but I apologized over and over and even put a Band-Aid on it. To this day, I don't know how Sheriff Grimme got that story.

"Sheriff Grimme was not easy to talk to. He was gruff and just this side of being rude. He scared me. But now I realize he had the murder of a seventeen-year-old girl staring him in the face, and everyone wanted answers."

Ann Reeves was another student called to the principal's office that memorable afternoon.

"I felt more embarrassed than anything to be called out of

class," Reeves said during a December 26, 2016, interview, "and everybody knew [that she'd been called out]."

She was unsure about what was going on, until the sheriff turned to her.

"He asked if I knew anything about Olene's disappearance," she said, "and if she had had any arguments with anybody. That kind of stuff."

Reeves explained that she had been with Olene the Friday before, "…just hanging together. Olene was passing notes back and forth to Tom Preston at the time, and I was the go-between. They had a *thing*."

About an hour after school had been dismissed that Monday, Olene's friend and classmate John O'Banion was sitting in his car at the Jim Dandy Drive-in, when he noticed Phil Nichols drive by in the Young-Nichols ambulance and pull into the alley next to the funeral home. Because of O'Banion's tight-knit relationship with the Emberton family, he felt duty-bound to go talk with Nichols.

"I went over and asked if that was about Olene," O'Banion recalled during an April 2017 interview.

Learning of Olene's death, he hurried back to his car and drove straight to the Emberton house. Upon arrival, he found the front door open and people "everywhere," shedding tears, expressing condolences, asking questions.

"Bobby [Olene's youngest brother who was then eleven] came running out to me, and he was crying." O'Banion said. "That was rough." •

This progression of family and school pictures shows Olene from a baby through age seventeen. Top row, from left: at about ten months, about age two, and grade three. Second row from left: seventh grade, eighth grade, and ninth grade. Third row from left, eleventh grade, age sixteen, and one of the poses she selected for her graduation photo. (Photos courtesy of Debbie Emberton.)

> *"Who really knew Olene? I didn't."*
> — Alice Cummins

6
WHO WAS OLENE EMBERTON?

Roxie kept all of Olene's belongings — including her school papers, letters, diaries, and photographs — partly out of sentiment and partly, as Marty Talbert speculated, because she held the belief that eventually the case would be reopened and something found in her daughter's possessions would hold the missing clue. Regrettably, Roxie's hope for closure never materialized, and after her death in 2011, her son, David, cleaned out the family home, pitching all but a handful of his sister's personal effects.

Thus, what is known about Olene has been pieced together from toneless legal documents and newspaper articles, and pried from the memories of those who knew her. In addition, much can be inferred from her own words recorded in an autobiographical essay written for school in 1963, when she was fifteen.

Olene's brief autobiography appeared in the November 22, 1965, *Kokomo Morning Times*. In it, she presented herself as a happy, thoughtful, upbeat girl with noble plans that, sadly, would never materialize. The essay read:

> "My name is Olene Emberton and I was born at Tompkinsville, Kentucky on December 17, 1947. After a few months my parents and I moved to a farm north

of Tipton, Indiana. We lived on the farm for two years. Then we moved into town and lived here for three years. Our present home is a farm west of Tipton. We have lived here for ten years.

"I am the eldest of the four children in our family. I am the only girl, also. My brothers are Floyd Wayne, 13; David Allen, 10; and Bobby Gene, 7. My father's name is Floyd Walter, and my mother's name is Roxie. No one else lives in our home with us.

"I have enjoyed knowing that my family likes to be a group instead of individuals. Some of my most fun has been being with my family. As for unhappiness in my life, I have not had any. I enjoy being with my family very much.

"I have many outdoor and indoor activities. I like to read books and listen to records. I'm in good health. Of course, I've had the childhood diseases. Once I was ill for a long time because I had the measles, whooping cough, and chickenpox too close together.

"Our family has not made many trips because living on a farm it's hard to get someone to take care of the livestock.

"My first three elementary school years, I went to Lincoln School. Then I was transferred to Jefferson School in the fourth grade. My favorite elementary school grade was the sixth. My best friends were Karen Sottong and Susie Clark. Our favorite grade school game was hopscotch.

"My first semester as a freshman in Tipton High was sorta hard, because of the grades I made in Latin. The second semester seemed a lot easier.

"I plan to graduate from high school in 1966. I want to attend Ball State University. After I graduate, I want to be a junior or high school teacher."

If Olene had lived to fulfill her dreams, she would have been the first in the Emberton family to graduate college.

Olene's friends knew her as a quiet, pleasant, and well-liked girl. The 1966 Tipton High School yearbook, the *Tiptonian*, included a small tribute to her. The cutline next to her photo reads:

> "On October 19 [sic], 1965, Olene Emberton met an untimely death. She was a prominent member of the senior class and ranked high scholastically at the time of her passing. Olene participated in FBLA [Future Business Leaders of America], GAA [Girls' Athletic Association], Latin Club, Foreign Language Club, Pep Club, and Yell Block. Her pleasing personality will be remembered by all."

Tipton High School Vice Principal Dorman Rogers spoke with the *Kokomo Tribune* on Wednesday, October 20, 1965. Based on his comments, the paper described Olene as quiet and businesslike, self-disciplined, and quite congenial.

Rogers said Olene was reserved but was one of the school's best students, ranking twenty-first in a class of one hundred eighty-five.

Ask members of the Tipton High School Class of 1966 today if they had known Olene Emberton well, and most will answer with a shrug or a headshake. Or both. For a girl who attended Tipton schools from kindergarten through grade twelve, surprisingly few of her classmates considered her a close friend. Even today, members of the T.H.S. Class of '66 described her as "a girl who was just there" and "a wallflower." One recalled her as so unremarkable that "she was like wallpaper."

Jennifer Cels remembered Olene as quiet. Vickie Porter agreed, adding that Olene also was polite and pleasant.

"And odd," said Karyn Roseberry.

"She never was in the limelight," said Jo Anna Powell.

"Who really knew Olene?" asked Alice Cummins. "I didn't."

Karen Ripberger said, "I think she was pretty elusive and nobody really knew her."

Wanda Abney felt much the same way. "I think she was a Jefferson (Elementary School) kid," Abney said, "but I don't remember her in any of my classes."

Neither did Jill Edgar, who attended first through third grade at Lincoln Elementary with Olene. "The only memory I have of Olene is talking to her on the playground and comparing our 'sack dresses,'" Edgar said, "which were all the rage."

Gail Wix was among the few who remembered Olene more clearly, first as a playmate at Jefferson after Olene transferred there from Lincoln and several years later as a rival, vying for the attention of the same boy.

"She was like the rest of us after she was there awhile," Wix wrote, referring to a very young Olene during their grade school years. "We all played together back then — jacks, hopscotch, jump rope. Those were good days."

Wix didn't always get along with Olene, however. During their junior year of high school, both girls began to date fellow classmate Tom Preston, and after that, she said, Olene realized she had competition and began to look at Wix but never speak.

"Looking back on those years," Wix continued, "I now wish we could have just looked at each other in the halls without being resentful. I truly wish that. ... I was never a best friend of Olene's, but I wish we hadn't been rivals. It has left me feeling a little guilty for not trying to work things out with her."

In late 2005, Dennis Murray, who had served as class president in 1966, sent an email in which he wrote about Olene. He was pleased to share his memories for use in a book that would one day be published about her. Murray died in 2009.

"I remember her as kind of shy and not very outspoken," Murray wrote, "but always willing to help on school projects when asked. My last memory of her, other than the funeral, was when we had the class down to Walt's [Murray's older half-brother, Walter Murray] barn, and all of us were decorating a float for homecoming. About twenty of the class members were there and we all had a good time.

"When she ended up missing and then was found dead on a country road, we all were in shock. I don't think she had an enemy in the world because she always was so pleasant — quiet but pleasant. That is about all I remember."

Ed Achenbach's memories weren't quite as vivid. He hadn't known Olene well, even though their families lived southwest of Tipton on farms not far apart. As students at Lincoln Elementary School, they had ridden the same school bus.

"I didn't like her much," Achenbach said almost apologetically, admitting that he remembered her as somewhat snobbish. "She would get on the bus and sit by herself."

Randy Horton shared Achenbach's assessment.

"My only memory of Olene was passing her in the hallway," Horton said. "I don't think I ever heard her talk. I never spoke to her. I thought she was unfriendly."

Jo Anna Powell, to the contrary, didn't view Olene's seemingly standoffish behavior as snobbish. Rather, Powell attributed it to timidity or a stymied self-confidence stemming from a home life that she suspected was oppressive. Powell based her assumption on an encounter she'd had with Olene in the spring of 1965.

She and Olene had never been close friends, but the two became better acquainted that spring as members of the Junior-Senior Prom Committee, spending several evenings together decorating the Tipton County 4H Building for the upcoming annual prom.

Powell didn't have a car, but Olene did. And because the two lived within two blocks of each other, Powell had hitched rides with Olene to the fairgrounds and back home. One night, according to

Powell, Olene had turned back the time on her dashboard clock, causing Powell to miss her ten o'clock curfew by an hour.

"I got in trouble," Powell said. "I told her my mom wasn't going to let me ride with her anymore, and Olene said, 'I don't want to get home until eleven.' I asked her, 'What are you so afraid of? Your brothers and your dad are there.' And she said she'd rather wait until her mom got home."

Powell never forgot that comment. It made her wonder if Olene was fearful of something at home — specifically, perhaps, her father.

Doris Morris, long-time Tipton resident and former head of nurses at Tipton Memorial Hospital, was Floyd Emberton's first cousin and knew him well. During a February 2017 telephone interview, Morris was adamant that Olene had nothing to fear at home.

"Floyd was strict," Morris said, "but he never abused her. She wasn't afraid of him. … He would have been angry if she didn't meet her curfew. He could get angry. But with most all the Embertons, there's a quick temper, but they didn't get physical. He adored her."

Ann Reeves also believed Olene's skittishness was grounded *not* in fear of her father but rather in burdens stemming from being the oldest sibling.

"Olene may have had to babysit for the young ones," Reeves said. "I think she had a lot of responsibility."

Although Olene had attended Tipton schools her entire life, Jim Harmon had no memory of her until their freshman year of high school.

"I assume she was at junior high school, too," he wrote in a 2017 email, "but I don't have any memories of her in seventh and eighth grade."

Harmon had forgotten that he and Olene were classmates as far back as fourth grade, evidenced by a school photo of all the students in Mrs. Thatcher's class posing on the steps of Jefferson School in 1958. In the photo, Harmon is kneeling directly in front of Olene.

Recalling her well during their high school years, however, Harmon wrote, "Olene and I were in a lot of classes together, and I remember her as being kind of quiet but very nice. She was very likable. She had a good sense of humor, and I remember teasing her from time to time. She always looked nice, and I remember her hair always being well kept."

Harmon continued, reflecting on his relationship with Olene — both in and outside the classroom.

"I would certainly consider Olene a friend," he wrote, "but we didn't hang out much together. We were just friends in class and around school. She was a very good student and probably helped me out in class a couple of times. I remember borrowing her notes in a couple of classes."

Mary Coan noted in a February 2017 email that she hadn't been a close friend of Olene's.

However, she explained, "She was nice, but shy, and didn't talk

Olene's fourth-grade class poses on the front steps of Jefferson Elementary School in the spring of 1958. Jim Harmon is shown kneeling second from left, directly in front of Olene. (Photo courtesy of Denny Speer.)

much. I think she was a good student and well liked. When I heard she was missing, I was totally shocked. She didn't seem to be the kind of girl that would run away, and really bad things just didn't happen in our little community."

Of all the members of the T.H.S. Class of '66 interviewed, Patricia Brooks perhaps had been closest to Olene because they both attended the Tipton Church of Christ.

"I met Olene during my high school years," Brooks wrote in her email. "I remember her as being quiet and smiling a lot."

Brooks learned from her parents that Olene had been found dead. "I was shocked that something like that could happen in our little town," she wrote. "It was so scary."

Olene's friend, Mollie Russell, remembered Olene as a bit moody.

"Sometime during that summer, Olene got very quiet," she said. "But Olene was the type who, when she wanted to talk to you, she would. If not, you left her alone. She was quiet. I can't say that I really knew her, even though we were together quite a bit.

"Olene wasn't close to people," Russell continued, "and I think that was because of her home life. Her mother was a worker. They had that mobile home park, and she was out working with Floyd — mowing, cleaning up."

According to Doris Morris, her own mother, Olean (who was Floyd's aunt), was the namesake for Floyd and Roxie's daughter. Morris spoke of one special memory of her young, second cousin that she cherished.

"Olene had come to my house selling magazine subscriptions," Morris said, "and I remember so well that I had Anita Bryant's record of *How Great Thou Art* playing. Olene and I stood there and listened to that, and she said, 'That's such a beautiful song.' And when they [the Emberton family] were deciding what music to play at the funeral, I told them Olene liked that song." •

> "It seemed like Olene's death shattered that family. They were never able to recoup. ... They loved her so."
> — Doris Morris

7
THE EMBERTON FAMILY

Floyd Emberton had been thirty-nine years old and Roxie thirty-six the day they received the news no father or mother should ever be asked to endure. Their beloved, only daughter had been found dead, and worse, there was no apparent reason, and worse yet, she may have been murdered. While their faith in God remained resolute, Olene's mysterious, unexpected death tested Floyd and Roxie's temperament, their marriage, their commitment to their family, and their ability to remain civil.

Before Olene's death hurled the Emberton family into the harsh limelight as a grieving family in shock, they had been nearly anonymous throughout Tipton County. Aside from the family's church involvement, the kids' school activities, and Floyd's work at Steel Parts, the Embertons were acquainted with relatively few Tipton residents.

John O'Banion, however, was an exception. O'Banion was a member of Olene's high school class, but it was his close friendship with her brother Floyd Wayne that spawned his relationship with the family. All the Embertons accepted him as a friend, and over time, he grew to love them as his surrogate family.

When O'Banion consented to an interview for this book in

early 2017, his lingering affection for the family was quite apparent.

O'Banion believed he met Floyd Wayne in 1963, when he was fifteen years old and Floyd Wayne was thirteen.

"It was before they moved into town," he said. "When I found out they had ponies, I got on my bike and rode out to their farm."

O'Banion said he had always remembered Floyd and Roxie as the hardest-working people he had ever known.

"When they lived on the farm, [Roxie] could pick a hundred hampers [of tomatoes] a day," he said. "She was strong. She had big

Roxie and Floyd, circa 1948 (Photo courtesy of Debbie Emberton.)

muscles. Olene's dad was the same way, always working. He always had some way to make money. When they lived in the country, they grew tomatoes … and hogs, which is not easy, and they had cows. Then when they moved to town, Floyd started that trailer park. It was all work, but usually Sunday was family day. People from Illinois would come over, and Roxie's sisters from Indianapolis. They had good family get-togethers."

Doing chores was a way of life for all the Embertons. The boys were always busy working outside, and Olene was always in the house cleaning and cooking, he said.

O'Banion said it wasn't unusual for Floyd to suddenly have all the kids start helping with a building project, and if O'Banion happened to be there, he was included.

"That's how it went with them," he explained. "You go over there, and you're going to be doing something. We didn't get paid — maybe some chocolate pie. But that was it, and it was kind of fun."

O'Banion called Floyd "a great guy."

"He was very strict, and a hard worker," O'Banion continued. "He'd get up at four-thirty in the morning, and Roxie got up and made breakfast. He worked all day at Steel Parts, and he'd get home about three o'clock and start working on his trailer court."

He even put up their house on Sweetland Avenue, O'Banion said.

"They built that house … in *one month*," he said, emphasizing his last two words. "It had three bedrooms. One of them was for Olene."

According to O'Banion, Floyd was highly intelligent, but he didn't know how to read. So, Roxie did the reading and writing.

"She was a heck of a business partner," he said.

Roxie was always ready to pitch in and help Floyd with whatever project he had going.

"Floyd would buy old trailers and put the A-frame roof on

Roxie, left, and her sisters — Joyce, Rose, Isabel, and Jonelle — pose with their mother, Fannie, while they display their handiwork following a family quilting bee, circa 1962. (Photo courtesy of Debbie Emberton.)

them," he said, "and Roxie could do it too."

She was also highly competent in the traditional duties of a homemaker.

"She had that sewing machine going all the time," O'Banion said. "She made comforters, doll clothes, and quilts. Then she'd have a garage sale. She also made fantastic chocolate pie."

O'Banion told a story that illustrated the difference in Floyd and Roxie's makeup and the way they related to the world. He had been at their house the evening of June 9, 1966, and observed Roxie open the *Tipton Tribune* and give it a look.

"'There was an article on the front page reporting that Tom [Preston] had been killed," O'Banion explained, "and when Roxie saw it, she wailed."

Olene had dated Preston for several months before her death, despite her father's wishes that his daughter date a Protestant boy rather than a Catholic with a questionable reputation. As Olene's friends recalled, her father's temper, when coupled with his intense dislike for his daughter's former boyfriend, was a potentially explosive combination.

"She showed the paper to Floyd," O'Banion continued. "Floyd threw it down and told her not to cry about Tom."

Floyd and Roxie lived conservatively and almost never spent money on luxuries or items they didn't need, even though, as O'Banion pointed out, they made a fairly healthy income buying trailers and renting them out. Regardless, O'Banion emphasized that he never saw any sign of marked extravagance.

"If Floyd made money, he put it back in the business," O'Banion said.

Floyd also sold used cars next door to the house. In fact, O'Banion said, that's how Floyd got the 1957 Chevrolet for Olene.

"He painted it [red] with a *paint brush!*" he said with slack-jawed astonishment. "I used to drive that thing. Floyd put a governor on the carburetor so it wouldn't go fast."

Like many young people, O'Banion moved out of Tipton following high school graduation in 1966 and started his life. He would never again make Tipton his home but returned often to visit family and friends. He remained close to the Embertons over the years, mourning the loss as each of them died.

Floyd was first. He died the morning of Saturday, July 4, 1981, of a self-inflicted gunshot wound, bringing an end to a three-year bout with cancer. He was fifty-four.

"That's just the way he was," O'Banion said, "a tough guy. He took things in hand."

Olene's youngest brother, Bobby Gene, was next, when he was killed in a car crash April 10, 1990. He was just thirty-four.

Roxie died May 3, 2011, due to cancer and complications related to Alzheimer's. She was eighty. Olene's middle brother, David, also died of cancer. He passed April 19, 2014, at the age of sixty-one.

Today, only Floyd and Roxie's firstborn son, Floyd Wayne, and their adopted daughter survive. However, he could not be located for comment, and she asked to be unnamed.

* * *

Debbie Arnett became an Emberton on March 11, 1972 — the day she married David.

Debbie had been seven years old, when she and the boy she would one day marry became acquainted at church. Both of their families considered the Tipton Church of Christ their home church, even though Debbie's family lived twenty-one miles south in Westfield.

"We began dating in 1970, when I was a freshman and Dave was a junior," Debbie said, reminiscing about happier times. "Dave got his brother Bobby to ask if I'd go to the prom with [David], so I did. Dave was too shy to ask for himself. We just started dating, and we dated continuously after that. We got married when I was a junior."

David was handy with tools and made repairs around the house, Debbie said. He was always close to his parents, and he was always available to help them out with the trailer court and the houses they bought and fixed up.

According to Debbie, Floyd and Roxie bought houses in need of repair, refurbished them, and then sold them.

"They flipped houses all over town," she said.

Floyd and Roxie provided David and Debbie a house on North East Street. They later built a house for Bobby across the street from their own home on Sweetland Avenue. David and Debbie moved into Bobby's house after he was killed.

Debbie recalls Floyd and Roxie with fondness, describing

them as loving grandparents to her children, as well as kind in-laws. Because Floyd lived only nine years after Debbie and David married, she didn't get the opportunity to know him as well as she had known Roxie.

Describing Floyd, Debbie said he was always working. "He worked on the farm and at Steel Parts, and when he got sick [in the early 1960s], the doctor said it was a heart attack and suggested he sell the farm."

As for Floyd's demeanor, Debbie said, "He always seemed really gruff. He wasn't one to talk much, but he was always helping us out. ... I remember once, after I'd had my first child [Shawn], Floyd was saying we needed another kid. Shawn was crying and Floyd was watching TV, so I put Shawn on his lap and said, 'Here, *you* take care of him,' and Floyd broke out in a little smile."

In this undated photograph, Floyd (left) receives a handshake and a gift from Steel Parts' Manager Bill Johnson. (Photo courtesy of Debbie Emberton.)

It had been typical for Floyd to keep his emotions undercover, but they were there, Debbie said, citing example after example of his good nature. Roxie, on the other hand, was not challenged on the emotions front.

"She sure did talk a lot," Debbie said with a laugh. "… and she was always making me something … and always buying me something … and would come over to clean my house. I think she was a workaholic. She had a good heart."

As for the way Roxie treated her grandchildren, "She spoiled them rotten," Debbie said, "and babied them."

Debbie, like John O'Banion, reminisced about Roxie's affinity for making quilts and chocolate pie.

"She had *so many* quilts," she said. "After she died, we divvied them up to the family. … And yes, she made good chocolate pie, but she was better known for her butterscotch pie … and chicken and dumplings."

Debbie described Roxie as a tiny woman, not much over five feet tall, and slender, not unlike her daughter.

"Roxie was probably a size six," she said, "a little woman but strong."

Relative to her size, her hands seemed too big, Debbie said.

"Roxie always hated her big hands," she said. "I think they were big because she worked so hard."

As can be expected, Roxie never got over Olene's death.

* * *

Former Howard County Sheriff Marty Talbert became acquainted with Roxie in 1993, while he was an Indiana State Police officer investigating the 1990 murder of a young woman in Porter County. A thread from that case led him to Tipton, specifically to Olene's unsolved death.

"I met [Roxie] at her home," Talbert said, during a conversation in February 2018. "As we talked, she recounted the circumstances of Olene's disappearance. She said, Olene was a good girl and didn't have a history of running away or juvenile problems, and not returning home was completely out of character for her."

Talbert continued, "Roxie appeared to have been haunted by her daughter's death and obviously wanted closure. ... She was friendly. She was glad somebody was still interested in the situation with Olene. Roxie took me to look at Olene's room, and I think it was just like she left it."

* * *

Roxie Blythe and Floyd W. Emberton married on June 15, 1946, in Tompkinsville, Kentucky, just thirteen miles north of the Tennessee line. She was fifteen; he was nineteen. Both were children of the Depression, both raised in abject poverty in Tompkinsville.

"[During the Depression] there were no jobs, no work for anyone," explained Floyd's cousin, Doris Morris during a 2018 telephone conversation. "In 1939, people couldn't feed their families. They stood in line for any work available through the WPA. It makes me cry to think about how that must have felt for people with pride.

"Boys didn't go to school," she continued. "They had to stand in line for work to help feed the family, but Floyd was too young for the jobs. That's why he came to Indiana, where he had two aunts."

One was his Aunt Alicia, and the other was Morris' mother, Olean. Floyd's father, Clarence, was their brother. After Floyd's family relocated to Indiana, she said, he lived part of the time with his Aunt Olean.

"He didn't read or write," she said, "but he was smart. He could do math, and he had a good, analytical mind. He was a good thinker and planner, even at a young age. When he left that rural Kentucky area to come to Indiana, he took any job he could do. He picked tomatoes, cleaned out barns, hauled off dung. He did anything."

Roxie and Floyd met as teenagers during the 1945 tomato-picking season in Tipton County. At the end of the season, Roxie returned to Tompkinsville with her family. It didn't take her long to decide to marry Floyd, and he rushed back to his hometown and to Roxie. The young couple said "I do" and embarked on the next chapter of their lives the following summer, optimistic and eager to start their own family.

"They were good people," Morris said. "They knew the pain of poverty, and they were determined to make a good life."

Olene, born in December of 1947, was still a baby when the Embertons came to Indiana looking for a better life.

"I saw this young mother with a baby she just adored," Morris said. "She was Roxie's doll baby. And Floyd thought she was the sweetest little thing and called her Little Tootie."

Floyd and Roxie welcomed their next child, Floyd Wayne, in 1949. Sadly, their next baby, a son, died shortly after his birth in 1951. But the births of two more sons helped mend their broken hearts — David in 1952 and Bobby Gene in 1955.

"My mother always had a link to Floyd," Morris said. "He was just so special to her, and she loved his children."

Morris shared her mother's deep affection for the children.

"Olene and her brother Floyd Wayne," Morris continued, "were the flower girl and ring bearer at my wedding."

Olene had been seven years old.

"I remember how responsible and capable she was," Morris said. "She was shy, very polite, and smiled a lot. I can remember Floyd watching her and Floyd Wayne with tears flowing down his cheeks. He was just really proud of his kids."

Morris and her husband, Ted, who was an officer at the Farmers Loan & Trust of Tipton at the time of the tragedy, provided support and advice to the Embertons in the days and weeks following Olene's death.

Morris had learned from her mother that Olene's body had

been found. "Floyd and Roxie were absolutely distraught," she said. "I just remember the hurt, the disbelief, and the questions — so many questions."

By then, Morris had been a registered nurse at Tipton County Memorial Hospital for several years. She recalled trying to comfort her cousin, Floyd, after he learned that an autopsy would have to be performed on his daughter.

"He said, 'No, you're not going to cut on her,'" Morris said. "I had to talk with him, tell him it had to be done, that it was the only way to find out what took Olene's life. He hated it."

It was painful, she said.

"Floyd felt that he had failed Olene," she continued, "and he could never understand how he could have let that happen. It seemed like Olene's death shattered that family. They were never able to recoup. There was nothing else they could talk about. They could never get her off their minds. They loved her so."

Looking back, Morris realized that after the family lost Olene, they withdrew into themselves, and she didn't speak with them as often as she once had. She's always wished there had been more she could have done to help them through their grief, although, even now, she isn't certain what that might have been.

"Who knows what you could have done?" she commented rhetorically. "The Embertons were a good family. They really had to believe that right wins out and that eventually [Olene's death case] would be solved. They just wanted to know."

She blamed Floyd's suicide on the lack of closure and his inability to cope with it.

"He just kind of shriveled up," Morris said. "It destroyed him. His family was his life." •

> *"I don't see any reason why this girl's not sitting here telling us what happened."*
> — Dr. James McFadden, pathologist

8
SHOCK ROCKS TIPTON

The Young-Nichols ambulance removed Olene's body from the crime scene at approximately 3:30 p.m. Monday, October 18 and transported it to the Leatherman-Morris Funeral Home. Dr. James McFadden, a fifty-three-year-old pathologist of Physicians Clinical Laboratory of Lafayette, Indiana, performed an immediate and complete autopsy.

Prior to joining Physicians Clinical Lab in 1956, McFadden had acquired twenty-three years of practical pathological experience, preceded by four years of university-level teaching. He also headed up the laboratory and pathology departments at Hendricks County Hospital in Danville, Indiana.

James Pratt, the Tipton police chief at the time of Olene's death, was present at the autopsy. During an interview at his home in October of 2006, Pratt talked about the procedure and the medical examiner's bewildering conclusion. Pratt explained the autopsy process he had witnessed more than forty years before. As he recalled:

> "The pathologist had his own nurse, who took all of the samples he handed her, and she would label each

one and set them down. He just started in and took out organs. He would take a biopsy of each organ, and he would examine it and lay it over to the side. He opened the skull up and examined the brain, and took the contents of the stomach.

"After he finished, he looked around and said, 'I don't see any reason why this girl's not sitting here telling us what happened.' He said the heart 'just quit.' There's no puncture wounds; there's no bruising; there's nothing to indicate what happened to her."

Pratt pointed out that, although the weather on the Sunday following Olene's disappearance was sunny and unseasonably warm, reaching at least eighty degrees, "Her body wasn't sunburned."

Thus, McFadden was able to make a safe assumption.

"He figured she was out there only a couple hours before the sun went down on Sunday afternoon," Pratt said. "She had been laid out there, and her clothes were neatly folded and lying beside her. No one's ever figured that one out yet."

The circumstances led Pratt to make an assumption of his own.

"Whoever she was with sure didn't want to be caught at the scene with her," he said. "In all probability, they would have had to haul her body around part of Sunday before they took it out there. So, somebody didn't have a conscience."

Pratt recalled the rumors that alleged Olene had choked on a foreign substance or was deliberately strangled. But as he pointed out, "McFadden checked her larynx and her voice box, and it was all intact. ... When he did the autopsy, he cut way up and stuck his finger up her neck and through her mouth, and he said, 'They're touching. There's nothing in there.' ... There was nothing in her throat. It was open. No bones were broken."

The doctor was baffled by the lack of evidence, Pratt said. And most surprising was McFadden's conclusion that Olene had not been raped, that her vaginal area was free of the type of injuries consistent with forced intercourse.

"There was no tearing or anything to indicate she had been raped," Pratt said. "But he [McFadden] stopped short of saying she hadn't had sex."

McFadden's determination wasn't the final verdict, however. As was customary, he forwarded the organs, along with tissue and blood samples to the Indiana University Medical Center and the Indiana State Police Crime Lab for further analysis. Her clothing also was sent to the state police lab to test for trace evidence, such as hair and semen, which, if detected, could help identify a suspect. A lot of hope was riding on the final results of the autopsy, toxicology, and physical evidence examination.

* * *

Fifty-plus years later, it's difficult not to wonder whether using the embalming room at the Leatherman-Morris Funeral Home to perform Olene's autopsy had hindered McFadden's ability to conduct it properly.

During a December 2017, phone interview, Tipton County's Coroner Brad Nichols said, "There's always a potential. It's much better to do it in a medical setting."

However, he added, "We're back to doing autopsies at the [Young-Nichols] funeral home."

He explained that autopsies had been performed for many years at Indiana University Health-Ball Memorial Hospital, but the hospital stopped the service for all outside counties in 2014.

"Tipton doesn't have a morgue," he said, "so we're performing autopsies at the funeral home. I'm satisfied with what we have. Although, it would be better if we had a better-engineered facility."

Nichols went on, "But I don't know if being in a facility would have enhanced the results [for Olene's autopsy].

What's of the foremost importance, he said, is the expertise of the person doing the autopsy.

"You need a pathologist," he said. "You lean on them. Their expertise really enhances the investigation."

* * *

The day after Olene was found — Tuesday, October 19 — page one of the *Tipton Tribune* displayed a seven-column-wide banner headline reading, "CLUES SOUGHT IN LOCAL SLAYING." It was the *Tribune*'s first story about the mysterious death of the "pretty blond Tipton High School senior ... described as a 'nice girl with a quiet disposition and not one to date a great deal.'"

The *Kokomo Morning Times* splashed a more graphic recap across its front page, reading, "TIPTON GIRL'S NUDE BODY IS FOUND." But the *Indianapolis Star* went with a less salacious "Missing Tipton Girl's Body Found in Ditch" headline to top its brief, but above-the-fold, two-column story.

Olene's death, as described by the same day's *Kokomo Tribune*, "remained shrouded in mystery Tuesday as authorities awaited a pathologist's report on the case."

Newspapers throughout the state reported the perplexing death, noting that forty-eight to seventy-two hours typically were required for the state to fully process the autopsy and issue the findings. They also stated that in the meantime, law enforcement officials were working all leads to determine the manner in which Olene Emberton had met her death; and that although officers had picked apart the crime scene looking for clues, they had turned up nothing. In the absence of physical evidence, police were questioning everyone, including students, who claimed to have information, no matter how insignificant it may have seemed.

The *Indianapolis News*' evening edition posted an update to the story under the headline, "2 Boy Friends of Slain Girl Guarded."

Speaking to the *Tipton Tribune* and other news organizations during a Tuesday morning press conference at the sheriff's office, Verl Grimme said, "We have to assume it's murder, although at the present time there is no official cause of death."

Indiana State Trooper Robert Zell added during the briefing that he had not ruled out the possibility of kidnapping.

Echoing what McFadden had surmised during the autopsy, Grimme said, "It appears the girl hadn't been moved after being placed there, and from all indications, there were no man-made marks on her body."

The only marks on her body, Grimme noted, were insect bites.

Grimme agreed with a suggestion at the news conference that because of Olene's tiny five-foot, four-inch stature and weighing little more than a hundred pounds, she easily could have been carried there. That was a real possibility because, as Grimme emphasized, "There was no evidence of violence at the scene. Her glasses were on the ground nearby. Part of her clothing was over her hair and the rest at the left side of her head."

Indiana State Trooper Earl Francis, who was a familiar figure throughout Tipton, was present at the news briefing. According to the *Tribune*, Francis spoke of the family's premonition.

"The family feared something had happened to her," Francis said. "All her relatives did."

Supporting the premonition, Chief of Police Jim Pratt added, "They all spoke of it."

In answer to questions about Olene's vehicle, Grimme told the press that the Embertons had become aware early Sunday morning that Olene's vehicle was parked near the Wiggins' home located in the four hundred block of North Green Street. The *Tipton Tribune* reported that several people had seen it, including Mrs. Robert Roudebush, whose son, Phil, had accompanied Olene to the movie Saturday night. According to the *Tribune*, "Mrs. Roudebush ... recalled seeing the car when she let Mrs. Wiggins out at her home late Saturday night. Mr. and Mrs. Wiggins [Mary and Roscoe] own Brigg's Restaurant, where Mrs. Roudebush is a cook on weekends, and they were returning home from work."

During a February 2017 telephone interview, Jennifer Cels, daughter of Mary and Roscoe Wiggins, spoke of the car parked outside her house the night Olene went missing. She explained:

> "I didn't remember what time I got home and hadn't noticed, and my mother got home about 12:30, which was normal. My father was home, and I had been watching *Invasion of the Body Snatchers*. My mother came home and mentioned that there was a car parked in front of our house, which was unusual. I looked out the window, and I thought it looked like the car of several people I knew.
>
> "When I got up the next morning and noticed the car, I thought it looked like Olene's. It was parked perfectly, and I thought it must have broken down. There was not a bit of concern in my head. The car was still there when I came home later, and I wondered why. I never saw anyone around the car until after they found her body. The police said they were going to leave the car there a few days, but I can't remember how long."

According to Grimme, the car had been thoroughly dusted for fingerprints, but as of the Tuesday morning press briefing, none of the people questioned had been fingerprinted.

The *Indianapolis Star* reported, "Investigators questioned 20 persons Monday, most of them high school classmates of the slain girl. Nothing was learned." •

> *"All I remember is seeing her face, hearing sobbing ... and wondering 'Why?'"*
> — Gail Wix

9
THE LONG WALK TO GOODBYE

"The students are taking this very, very hard," Tipton High School Principal Charles Edwards said, as the *Kokomo Tribune* reported on Wednesday, October 20. "First there was doubt," he continued. "Then confusion. Then disbelief. But Wednesday morning, the real impact hit the teenagers."

Late that morning, Edwards led a group composed of approximately seventy-five of Olene's classmates, teachers, and underclassmen on an eight-block walk. Departing the school, they headed north along Main Street, passed through the downtown area, and proceeded until they reached the Leatherman-Morris Funeral Home at 314 North Main. There they would pay their respects to Olene, where her remains had been prettied-up, dressed, and displayed to await her funeral and burial that afternoon. The temperature that autumn morning hovered at a chilly sixty degrees, while a gloomy, overcast sky reflected the cheerless mood of the procession.

"We had to walk as a group in the drizzle is how I remember it," said Shirley Huss.

That's also how Floetta Scelta remembered it, as she noted in a February 2017 email. "Everyone was quiet. I think it was raining," she wrote, "or overcast."

Bill Tidler, on the other hand, remembers the weather that morning as "unusually nice" and the march to the funeral home as "almost surreal."

None of the students joked or laughed as they made their way up Main Street, Gail Wix recalled. Everyone was unusually quiet, she said, and some cried.

Jennifer Cels and Vickie Porter remembered the walk as somber.

Jo Anna Powell said that when the students arrived at the funeral home, they were instructed to enter through the back door.

"There's a little hallway and a big archway," Powell explained. "The casket sat on the west wall of that big room, and the way the flowers were, you had to go around to get to the casket. The boys went first."

The naïve seventeen- and eighteen-year-olds quietly filing into the viewing room were entering a scene that most were ill-equipped to cope with. Each was filled with apprehension. None had experienced the death of a peer before, and most were uncertain of how to feel, how to act, or how to properly express their condolences to the Emberton family. None expected the reception they encountered. Most were shocked, not merely because of what they saw, but because of what they heard.

Olene's parents were out of their minds with grief. They had already buried an infant son, Jerry, in 1951, and now they were burying their only daughter. They were obviously and understandably distressed, but that didn't make the situation any less alarming to the students.

Roxie was sobbing fiercely. As each girl approached, Roxie moaned, "Why couldn't it be *you*? Or *you*? Why couldn't it have been *you*?"

The boys fared no better than the girls. As they lined up in the hall waiting their turn, Floyd Emberton paced like a caged tiger. Sizing up each boy passing by, Floyd caught their eye and brusquely asked, "Was it *you*?" … "Was it *you*?" … "Do *you* know who did this to my daughter?"

Explaining what she had witnessed that day, Jo Anna Powell continued, "Mr. Emberton said — and this is what got me ... I had nightmares — he said to the guys going through, 'Did *you* do it? Did *you* do it?' And I'm thinking, 'What on earth?' Of course, I felt sorry for Roxie, but she was lying on the couch, and as we girls went through, she said, 'Why couldn't it have been *you*? Or *you*?' I knew she was distraught, but…"

Bill Tidler said he has always been bothered by the way Olene's mother reacted when she saw her daughter's classmates coming into the viewing room.

"I was among the first to enter the room, and Mrs. Emberton became hysterical, shouting and almost out of control," Tidler recalled.

Patricia Brooks wrote, "[Olene's] mom and dad were so heartbroken. She was their only girl. … Her mom was so distraught and crying loudly. I still remember hearing her."

Floetta Scelta said she also was struck by the chaos in the viewing room that morning. She explained:

> "I remember we entered from the side door, and when we walked in, the casket was on our right and the family pew was on the left. We were supposed to turn to our left just past the family. When we were in front of the mother, she said, and I quote, 'I've asked God a thousand times: Why wasn't it one of these girls instead of my daughter?'
>
> "That statement has stuck with me my entire life. I was shocked she would say that. She was a Christian, attending the same church as my family, so I couldn't believe a Christian would say something like that, even in grief. I think that was the beginning of my doubts in that church."

Terry Conwell also spoke of the awful scene she witnessed at Olene's visitation.

"I remember what her mother said," Conwell declared, "and I'll never forget it. She definitely said, 'Why did it have to be *my* kid? Why couldn't it be one of these *other* kids?' Of course, I understand she was distraught. Who wouldn't be? But you always remember if you heard something like that."

Vickie Porter also recalled the terrible scene she witnessed inside the funeral home that day. In an early 2017 email, she wrote:

> "Viewing Olene, for some of us, was one of our first encounters with death. Since Olene had been exposed to the elements, she barely resembled herself, which in itself was shocking. The most difficult thing for me was her mother shouting, 'Why couldn't it have been one of you?' Those words rang in my ears all the way back to school, and I have recalled them every time I have thought of this tragedy. As a young girl, I could not understand why she would say that; as an adult, I understand her grief."

As the students filed by, they looked away from the two inconsolable parents, but they couldn't block out the voices. The alternative was to look at Olene.

Typically, if the deceased had lain unprotected outdoors for several hours, their coffin would be closed. Olene's parents, however, chose to keep the coffin open for the viewing. As the students filed past, they were somber, silent, and ill at ease. Considering the circumstances, seeing Olene in death was traumatic enough for the impressionable teenagers.

The body in the frilled casket bore little resemblance to the pretty, fresh-faced teenager the students had known. Most were unnerved by Olene's unnatural appearance. In life, she had been slender and fair complected. In death, her body was bloated, and her skin had darkened, appearing somewhat leathery. It was speckled with blotchy patches and insect bites. Her hands, instead of resting peacefully on her midsection, were talon-like, splayed in front of her.

Jennifer Cels recalls entering the funeral home and sensing a "very deep" sense of sadness.

"And when I saw Olene," she said, "I thought she looked awful. I probably had never seen a dead body before, but it looked fake, and I didn't like it."

No one liked looking at their deceased school friend, and a number of Olene's former classmates specifically commented on the thoughts and feelings they had experienced that morning as they filed past her.

Ann Reeves recalled, "I couldn't believe somebody my age was dead."

Shirley Huss agreed, explaining, "It was the first corpse I had ever seen that was my age. For our age, it wasn't just a horror … it was unheard of."

Gail Wix felt much the same way.

"It was hard to look at [Olene]," Wix said, "knowing she was our age. She should not have been lying there. I don't remember what she was wearing. Nor do I care. All I remember is seeing her face, hearing sobbing, the smell of the funeral home, and wondering, 'Why?'"

Referring to the drab, sheer, dark-colored nightgown that Olene was buried in, Karen Brown said, "They had her dressed in something like a negligee. I couldn't understand why they'd dress someone so young like that."

Regardless of the undertaker's efforts to make Olene look attractive and natural, Jo Anna Powell offered details about the condition of Olene's body, which clearly showed the effects of exposure to the elements.

"They were very prominent," Powell said, also noting that Olene appeared to be swollen. "Oh, yes, about three times her size, so there was no way they could put her own clothes on her. So she had a nice negligee outfit, and they had actually bent her glasses to fit on her face."

Adding to that, Terry Conwell said, "I thought Olene looked real bad. She was just too big. Swollen. She didn't look right. At that time, we hadn't gone to a mortuary very much. You didn't expect somebody from your class to die. If they'd been sick, you could've prepared for it … but just overnight … it's not something you think is going to happen to you. It was a shock."

* * *

Floyd Emberton's cousin, Doris Morris, also attended Olene's visitation and vividly remembers the chaos that permeated the room as the students passed through.

"I was there, trying to console Roxie and get her calmed down," Morris explained. "There was not enough time for Floyd and Roxie to be alone with their daughter before the class came in. As I look back, I think there were too many people allowed in. It was too early. The whole class coming down was great, but the timing was lousy."

The family needed privacy, she said. Their time alone with Olene before the visitation was not sufficient for them to gather their composure.

In addition, she said, the Embertons hailed from a Southern culture, which compelled those who were grieving to display their emotions openly, without reservation.

* * *

Olene's funeral was supposed to begin at 2:00 p.m. Wednesday. However, due to the late arrival of the minister, the Rev. Eulon Knox, who had been vacationing in Florida, the service was delayed until four o'clock. Olene was buried in Tipton's Fairview

Cemetery.

The service was well attended and included many of Olene's school friends, teachers, and officials. Principal Charles Edwards told the *Kokomo Tribune* that the Tipton High School students were stunned.

"They still cannot believe that a thing like this could have happened here," he said. •

10
AUTHOR'S POINT OF VIEW: THE VIEWING

I was part of the contingent, which made the promenade through town that dreary, long-ago, mid-October morning to say goodbye to our classmate. My memory of the experience is sketchy, so I'm grateful that many old friends who also made the trek were able to fill in the details I'd forgotten. However, the few impressions I've retained of the incident remain vivid, playing like old movie scenes that flicker across my mind.

Looking back, I think as we processed up Main Street, we must have been quite a sight — an unusually solemn delegation of naïve teenagers, headed for the rudest awakening of our young lives.

As we passed quietly through town, I'm sure I wasn't the only one without a clue to what awaited us. I was seventeen, and at that point in my life, I had seen only one dead person, and that had been when I was five years old, and the deceased was an elderly woman I'd barely known. But that day — October 20, 1965 — I was about to see a dead classmate, the first in our class to make the transition. Nothing could have prepared me for the grueling scene I would soon witness.

I conducted a phone interview in September of 2004 with Keith Porter, who, as an employee of Leatherman-Morris Funeral

Home, had prepared Olene for burial. The thirty-nine years since her death was a long time, he said, thus he could not recall whether he had noticed marks on her body that would have been consistent with trauma.

"Things like that, I didn't pay attention to," Porter said. "Nobody that's dead looks nice, but I've always done everything I can to make them look nice.

"Things don't stand out in my mind," he continued. "She was a whole person and there was nothing for me to see. When I got done, she was the pretty little girl that she always was."

I received my first shock when I stepped into the mortuary parlor and realized that Olene's casket was open. The poor girl had lain in a patch of weeds for hours, exposed to nature's elements. But there she was, prepared for the viewing, dressed in a filmy, sterling silver-colored nightgown. Its long sleeves tapered to lacy ruffles that partially obscured the greenish-purple discoloration on the backs of her hands that now looked more like the hands of a department store mannequin than the soft, smooth hands of a seventeen-year-old girl. The gown's choker neckline unfurled below her chin in a cascade of graceful fabric that failed its obvious intended purpose: to flatter her pretty face.

None of us expected what came next.

Customarily, families of the deceased are afforded private time with their loved one before guests begin to arrive to allow them an opportunity to try to process the stark reality. Unfortunately, in Olene's case, it appeared that her family had arrived only minutes before our class. Without adequate time to adjust to seeing their daughter in death, Roxie dissolved into hysterics. I'm certain I felt pity for her, but I couldn't possibly have understood the excruciating anguish she was forced to endure and put on display for a roomful of her deceased daughter's friends.

Why *couldn't* it have been one of *us*? Why did it *have* to be *her* daughter?

Unlike so many of my former classmates, I either forgot or didn't hear Roxie repeatedly cry out those questions directed to the girls filing past Olene's casket. What I do remember, and what is permanently etched into my memory, is Roxie lying prostrate on a row of metal folding chairs (unlike Jo Anna Powell's memory of Roxie lying on a sofa), crying and moaning uncontrollably, surrounded by loved ones trying to comfort her.

As Terry Conwell noted, the events at Olene's viewing were a shock. Indeed, it was for those of us passing through. But for Olene's grief-stricken parents, it was an unthinkable, unbearable, heartbreaking blow from which they would never recover. •

> "*If you could see that mother and father down at the funeral home, you would understand why something needs to be done.*"
> — Emberton relative

11
MEANWHILE BACK AT THE JAIL

Shock seeped into the entire Tipton community. Everyone was eager for the case to be solved. As long as the person responsible for Olene's fate remained unidentified and free, parents would fear for the safety of their children. People looked at each other with an unfamiliar unease. Anyone could be a suspect.

A *Kokomo Tribune* reporter strolled through downtown Tipton the afternoon of Tuesday, October 19 intent on capturing the mood and the local scuttlebutt. The page one story in the next day's paper painted a picture of a town on edge, quiet, and melancholy, with small groups of residents congregating on street corners and inside shops. They were talking about Olene Emberton's tragic, mysterious death. They were concocting theories.

According to the *Kokomo Tribune*, an elderly woman standing in front of Citizens National Bank said to a friend, "Isn't it terrible? I still cannot believe that it happened. It's just awful."

Up the street, in one of the dimly lit, smoke-filled cigar stores — Frisz's most likely — a number of retired gentlemen sat around a large table playing cards.

"It's the weirdest mystery I've heard of in a long time," one of the men said past his mouthful of chewing tobacco.

Around the corner and two blocks over, a waitress at one of

the town's lunch counters — the Little Gem Café perhaps — was more specific.

"Many of us are just certain it had to be someone the girl knew well," she said as she wiped the marble countertop with a dishrag. "Everything just adds up to it. We've never had anything this terrible happen before." Shaking her head, she added, "They'll never find out what killed her … they'll never find out."

The Wednesday, October 20 *Indianapolis News* reported that members of Olene's family attended a briefing with local law enforcement authorities at the sheriff's office the morning before her funeral visitation. The story stated that the family offered what they thought might be leads. Grimme, in response, assured them that he was doing everything he could, prompting the family to express their frustrations and Floyd Emberton to storm out of the office in tears.

The paper quoted an unidentified Emberton relative as saying, "If you could see that mother and father down at the funeral home, you would understand why something needs to be done." And throughout Tipton, wrote the *Indianapolis News*, "residents' typical reaction to the mysterious murder was, 'You expect that sort of thing to happen in a big city, but in a town like Tipton?'"

Members of the news media were also present for the briefing, and they dug in with pen and notepad in hand, eager to record any and all tidbits of information they could extract from the Tipton County sheriff.

Grimme told them that the search for clues in the death had been intensified, stretching into the four surrounding counties — Clinton, Howard, Hamilton, and Madison. Every lead had been checked and rechecked, he said, and more than fifty persons had been interviewed, including at least twenty of Olene's friends. Grimme said a few inconsistencies had been detected in some of the answers, so to clear up the discrepancies, some of the individuals might be questioned again, and in some cases, lie detector tests may be necessary.

Chief of Police Jim Pratt said the two boys who had been held in protective custody had been released Tuesday afternoon. Neither boy had been a suspect, he said, but police did their due diligence and checked out the boys' stories, which had been substantiated by witnesses.

Grimme revealed that Olene's purse, containing her car keys, had not yet been found.

"We want that purse," he told the *Kokomo Tribune*. "It may not tell us a thing, but so far, it is the only thing we can find missing from the girl's personal effects."

Grimme also updated reporters about finger and palm prints lifted from Olene's car, according to the Kokomo paper. He said hopes were high that the prints would lead investigators to a suspect and possibly an arrest.

"From the quality of the markings we obtained," he said, "we believe the girl was lured from her auto by an acquaintance she had confidence in. All indications show there was no struggle when Miss Emberton left the car."

The sheriff said that it was his belief Olene had met another acquaintance after she drove away from the Roudebush home at 11:30 Saturday night.

"She would not have gone out to that area with someone she did not know," he said.

Grimme told reporters he would be sending the prints to the Indiana State Police Central Records office in Indianapolis and the F.B.I. in Washington, D.C., for possible identification.

"The investigation is being conducted under the assumption that the girl was murdered," Grimme continued.

However, the exact cause of death wouldn't be known until Indiana University Medical Center released the results of the pathology and toxicology tests. Investigators also were eager to see the outcome of the Indiana State Police Crime Lab's testing on

Olene's clothing.

Until investigators received the verdicts from the medical center and the lab, Grimme said, they would keep on "working the case from all other angles."

In wrapping up the briefing, he informed reporters that officers were in the midst of a house-to-house canvas of the neighborhood in which Olene's car had been found.

"Besides the purse, there is a missing link in our chain," Grimme asserted. "We think that the widespread search could help us determine where the girl was between 11:30 p.m., when she was last seen, and the time of her death.

"We are not discounting any possible clue. We are carrying out this thing around the clock and won't slow up until we tie up some of the loose ends." •

> *"Until we get the results of those tests, all we can look for is someone who illegally disposed of a body."*
> — Sheriff Verl Grimme

12
BRICK WALL

Despite the confidence the sheriff projected to the press, by Thursday, October 21, day four of the investigation, Grimme still had no evidence, clues, witnesses, motives, valid tips, or a cause of death. His team had hit a brick wall. He was desperate for valid information, as well as the test results from the Indiana University Medical Center and the Indiana State Police Crime Lab.

"We are still checking out all possible leads but seem to be following a blind road," he told the *Kokomo Tribune* on Thursday. "We hope the blood tests, skin specimens, or the clothing will give us a new road to follow in the investigation."

On Friday, Grimme received the first of the state toxicologist's test results. It confirmed that Olene's blood was free of alcohol. The report didn't tell him much else, but as reported by the *Indianapolis Star* on Friday, October 22, it was enough to compel him to say, "We are not discounting the possibility that she could have died of natural causes."

Like the *Star*, that day's *Indianapolis News* also reported Grimme would not rule out natural causes and that the person she was with dumped her body unclothed in hopes of "clouding" the investigation. The story continued, quoting Grimme as saying, "We still do not know whether we have a murder on our hands or not. ... Until we get the results of those tests, all we can look for is someone who illegally disposed of a body."

According to the *Indianapolis News*, Grimme had ruled out the theory that a stranger passing through Tipton had forced Olene into a car and killed her. As he had stated previously to the *Kokomo Tribune*, he believed she knew the culprit because her body revealed no signs of violence or resistance.

When the *Indianapolis News*' reporter asked Grimme if the death could remain a mystery in a small community like Tipton, where people were familiar with each other, Grimme said, "You'd think it couldn't, but I don't know."

The Thursday, October 28 edition of the *Kokomo Tribune* again reported that Grimme would not discount the possibility of natural causes.

"I'm leaving the door open to that line of thought until I get the reports," he told the Kokomo paper. "Even if something like that should show up, I can't close the investigation. I still have to know who the girl was with the night of her death."

Grimme continued, asserting that if Olene had become ill that night and subsequently died of related natural causes, "the person the girl was with had moral responsibilities to attempt to get her to a doctor or hospital if they were aware she was ill."

On the tenth day after Olene's body had been found, Grimme was no closer to determining what happened than he was on day one. However, according to the October 28 *Tipton Tribune,* as Grimme awaited the autopsy's long-awaited final report, he projected optimism that it would reveal the cause of death, which would point the way to new areas to investigate. The same day's *Tribune* also reported that State Police Sergeant Robert Zell had indicated that as soon as the new findings were released, his department would make available as many additional detectives as needed.

Unfortunately, on day eleven — Friday, October 29 — the report finally arrived, and all hope was crushed.

#T9 143

Coroner's Verdict

On the body of Olene Emberton

336 Sweetland Tipton, Ind.

held Oct 18 Testherman

JAN 21 1966
ROSS M. HUFFORD
CLERK TIPTON C. C.

Chester Mitchell
Coroner Tipton County, 1

The following is a description of the person over whose body the inquest was held:

Name: Olene Emberton
Usual Residence: 886 Sweetland Ave Tipton, Indiana
Birthplace: _____ Date of Birth: _____
Color or Race: white   Citizen What Country: USA
Age: 17   Sex: Fe   Height: 5-5   Weight: 105   Teeth: Natural
Color of eyes: Blue   hair: Brown   Complexion: Medium   Marital: Single
Occupation: Scholar   Marks: _____
The clothing was: Body was nude. Her clothes lay near the body

and had on h.... person at the time of h.... death

that came into my hands as Coroner.

In Testimony Whereof, I have hereunto set my hand and the seal of my office this 18th day of Oct., 19 65.

(Seal)   Chester Mitchell

Coroner Tipton County, Ind.

Tipton County Coroner Chester Mitchell filed his official verdict on January 21, 1966: "Reported cause of death undetermined." Above: Coroner's Verdict, Side 1. Facing page: Coroner's Verdict, Side 2. (Official court record, Tipton County Clerk's Office.)

I, Chester Mitchell   Coroner of said County, having examined the body of _____

a person whose death was supposed to have been caused by unlawful or suspicious means, had been found within said county. I hereby certify that I took charge of the remains described below and held an (inquest, autopsy, inquiry). After having heard the evidence, examined the body, and considered the facts and circumstances, I do find that the said deceased came to Her death by _____

at ____ M., _____ 19 __ at _____ .

The disease or condition directly leading to death was
Miss Emberton was last seen alive at 11:)00 P.M. Oct.16
~~Antecedent causes due to~~ Found At 2P.M. Mon 18th 2½ Miles N.E. of Hobbs Body ~~nude taken by Younge Ambulance to Tipton Body posted at the~~ Leatherman-Morris Funeral Home by Dr McFadden.

~~Other significant conditions~~: Dr McFadden (Pathologist) Dr Forney (Toxecologist) Reported cause of ~~Death undetermined.~~

I administered the usual oath to said witnesses

The deceased was (~~accompanied~~) or (found by): Mrs Donald Clouser
                                               R.R.#1 Windfall, Indiana

The place of injury was

and located
the time was   M.   19
The injury occured

* * *

Before making a public announcement, Grimme called for a meeting with involved officials — Tipton County Coroner Chester Mitchell, Medical Examiner Dr. James McFadden, Tipton Police Chief Jim Pratt, Tipton County Prosecutor Richard Regnier, Indiana State Police Detective Albert Merkle, and Dr. George Compton of Tipton. The meeting at the Tipton County Memorial Hospital lasted three hours. Afterward, Grimme called a news conference at which he released this bulletin:

> A pathologist report was delivered today to Chester Mitchell, coroner of Tipton County, regarding his findings in the death of Miss Olene Emberton. His final diagnosis was "cause of death undetermined."
>
> Other findings reported from the State Police Laboratory showed no presence of harmful drugs or alcohol in her blood. Tipton County Sheriff's Department, Tipton City Police, and state authorities continue to work to determine the cause of the mysterious death of Miss Emberton.

When a reporter asked Grimme if the findings were unusual, he snapped, "That's putting it mildly!"

The findings were a huge disappointment for the entire community and left Grimme with nothing more to pursue. A few days later, on November 4, Grimme told the *Kokomo Morning Times* that unless the person involved in Olene's death became conscience-stricken and confessed, solving the case was essentially hopeless.

In a December 7, 1965, interview with the *Kokomo Tribune*, Dr. James McFadden attempted to explain why Olene's official cause of death had to be listed "undetermined."

"In one to two percent of the cases I have worked on," he said, "it has been impossible to determine the cause of death. ... Being unable to determine the cause of death does not happen often, but on the other hand, it is not a medical rarity."

McFadden spoke of known causes of death that were difficult, if not impossible, to identify, such as fright. Although rare, he said, people have died of fright, and when they do, there is nothing in an autopsy that indicates what happened.

He went on to say there also were authenticated cases of people, especially athletes, having died of extreme physical effort, and another cause of death impossible to identify is suffocation.

"When babies pull those plastic bags over their heads and suffocate," McFadden said, "an autopsy does not give any evidence as to how they died."

* * *

A September 2004 phone interview was conducted with Dr. Robert Forney, Jr. His father, by then deceased, had been the toxicologist for Indiana University Medical Center that conducted the toxicology analysis on Olene's case. When the conversation turned to cause of death, Forney concurred with McFadden about the rarity but reality of undetermined causes of death.

"By the way," Forney said, "there is a certain percentage of cases that are simply never solved. It doesn't mean that people are incompetent."

In his December 2017 phone interview, Tipton County Coroner Brad Nichols confirmed both doctors' assertions regarding the unusual, but valid "undetermined" cause of death.

"To not find the cause is very infrequent," he said. "It's very, very rare." •

> *"He was crazy.*
> *He wasn't afraid of nothing."*
> — Retired Tipton Police Officer Randy Horton

13
WHO WAS VERL GRIMME?

McFadden's mini lecture about Olene's autopsy, as reported by the December 7, 1965, *Kokomo Tribune*, may have been technically informative, but it didn't satisfy the people close to her or the Tipton community. They wanted hard answers. In the absence of answers, they made up their own. Rumors were out of control, and most of them stemmed from their belief that Grimme lacked the experience to handle a case of such magnitude, despite the fact he was being assisted by topnotch detectives with the Indiana State Police.

The prevalence of that attitude begged the question: Was Verl Grimme a competent, confident but easygoing, "Mayberry RFD" Andy Taylor kind of sheriff, or a self-aggrandizing, bumbling, Barney Fife with anger issues?

Stories describing Verl Grimme — sometimes as an Andy Taylor *and* sometimes a Barney Fife — have circulated throughout the Tipton community for decades. However, the opinion carrying the most weight is the one shared unanimously by the professional law enforcement personnel who worked with him: Tipton County Sheriff Verl Grimme was a dedicated, professional public servant, who wanted nothing more than to figure out why Olene had died and who had abandoned her body along that secluded country lane.

It can't be emphasized too strongly that by the time Olene died,

Grimme already had acquired six years of solid law enforcement experience. He served four of those years as a deputy under his brother Paul Grimme, Tipton County sheriff from 1955 through 1958. After waiting out a term, he ran for sheriff in 1962 and won. It was his first of two consecutive, four-year terms as Tipton County sheriff.

"Verl was, at that time, a typical country sheriff," said retired Indiana State Police Officer Robert Zell during his 2006 interview.

Verl Grimme, Tipton County Sheriff 1962-1970 (Courtesy Diane Grimme Henderson.)

Zell had worked with the sheriff since the early 1950s, when Grimme launched his law enforcement career under his brother Paul As Verl Grimme's trusted friend and colleague, Zell was the first officer he called after arriving at the site where Olene's body had been found.

"Verl was very conscientious in what he did," Zell continued, "but he had very little, if any, formal training in law enforcement."

It was not unusual in the post World War II years for newly hired police officers and newly elected sheriffs to step into their jobs with no experience under their belts, he said.

"There was no police academy in Indiana at that time for city police or sheriffs," Zell explained. "Most of them did not have any formal police training."

Former Illinois State Trooper, Law Enforcement Intelligence Unit Agent, and State Police Detective Charles E. Neuf writes in his 2011 book, *State Police Trooper Action Short Stories*, "Policing in the 1950s and '60s was primitive in comparison to the modern policing of today."

In those days, according to Neuf, a candidate running for sheriff needed only a high school diploma or a G.E.D., physical stamina, and a willingness to work endless hours for low pay. Neuf's claim is substantiated by a page-five political advertisement in the November 4, 1960, *Tipton Tribune*, which reports the sheriff's pay at $5,300 annually.

In the absence of a semester-long course at a training academy, according to Neuf, inexperienced, new sheriffs nearly always relied on knowledge gained during ride-alongs with established, on-duty officers. Neuf states that during the 1950s and '60s, smaller departments often lacked resources and good communication equipment, forcing sheriffs to rely on their own judgment and split-second decisions.

"But," as Zell further explained, "[Grimme] was a hard worker and was honest, as far as I know, and did the very best he could."

Zell praised Grimme for his willingness to reach out to his Indiana State Police counterparts whenever he needed help.

"Verl was very confident," Zell explained, "and if he needed help, he called for help. He tried to get it from wherever it was available. When he saw he was in over his head, he wanted people in there who knew what they were doing."

Zell's recollections were nearly identical to those of Grimme's youngest sibling, Beryl Grimme.

"All the state policemen up there were very fond of Verl," Beryl said during a 2005 interview. "All he had to do was ask, and they would do it for him. And vice-versa. If they needed something, he would get it for them."

Michael Colgate, a former Indiana State Police Officer, got his start in law enforcement as a deputy under Grimme and was quite familiar with his former boss' attitudes and practices. Colgate wrote in a 2006 letter that, "Some local sheriffs' offices do not want the state police involved with *their* investigations. Tipton County at that time was not one of those. Verl wanted other agencies notified when things happened."

* * *

Verl Dietz Grimme was born November 8, 1915, in Indianapolis to Frank and Lillian Dietz Grimme, the third of eight Grimme children — six sons, two daughters — Paul, Leonard, Verl, Mary Elizabeth (Betty), Malcolm, Frank, Beryl, and Joy.

Grimme was a pleasant-looking man with a trademark, pencil-thin mustache and short-cropped brown hair that turned grayer with each passing year. Standing five-foot, six-inches tall, trim and solidly built, he was of average stature. Yet he projected an inner strength that could be downright off-putting and an unpredictable disposition that fluctuated according to the situation.

"He was mild-mannered," said Beryl Grimme, describing his brother, "but you wouldn't want to cross him. I found out that a little, short person always has more of a temper than a big, tall guy. He was just like that."

Grimme's parents met in Indianapolis on the streetcar Frank drove, and on which Lillian was a frequent passenger. After Frank finally asked Lillian out, they went on their first date at her father's dance hall, Dietz Grove. Frank and Lillian married in 1910 and moved to Tipton County near Hobbs in 1916, the year after Verl was born. The family later moved to Prairie Township, where Verl grew up and attended school. A popular student, Verl was active in sports — baseball and basketball mainly — but not always without setbacks.

Grimme was eighteen when he lost a few front teeth during a September 27, 1933, baseball game between Prairie and Windfall high schools. According to the *Tipton Tribune*, Prairie teammate Carl Shuck was at bat and struck a fast one, "swinging with all his might." That's when the bat slipped from his hands and flew over his head, striking Grimme in the face. While, the *Tribune* story ended with a note that Prairie lost the game 3 to 5, in terms of runs, the report may also have inadvertently referred to Grimme's personal loss, in terms of teeth.

Throughout his teens and early twenties, Grimme was also engaged in safer forms of recreation such as local talent shows, sometimes performing as a member of the chorus and other times as the master of ceremonies. He must have relished the shows for providing him an outlet for his hidden show-biz talents. For example, in January 1942, Chicago-based radio station WLS sponsored a talent show in the Prairie High School auditorium. The show, "Prairie Entertainment," featured a cast of no less than fifty local performers, with Grimme at the helm as emcee delivering his prized impersonation of Hollywood cowboy-movie sidekick Pat Buttram. More than seven years later, he was still generating laughs, as *Tipton Tribune* columnist R.D. Maney noted in his August 16, 1949, piece: "Verl Grimme should be 'cute' as Gene Autry ... he is a 'bus jockey' of no mean ability. Of course that voice of his is more on the 'bathtub' side than soap opera ... but he'll make it ... I hope."

Verl made his living as a truck driver after he graduated Prairie High School in 1934 and had been doing quite well. But World War II broke out, and like most healthy, stout-hearted, young, American men — members of what is now known as "The Greatest Generation" — Grimme stepped up, laying his life on the line for his country.

The June 16, 1942, *Tipton Tribune* carried a page one story reporting, "Forty-seven Tipton County men, ranging in age from 20 to 45, left for examination and possible U.S. Army induction at Fort Benjamin Harrison, Indianapolis, Tuesday morning, in one of the largest contingents to leave this county since the birth of the Selective Service System." The story listed names and addresses of the forty-seven men. The first was "Verl Dietz Grimme, Route 1,

Sharpsville."

During the war years, it was the *Tribune*'s practice to run updates almost daily to keep its readers informed on the whereabouts, activities, and status of the Tipton County men and women in service to America, as well as to share the cards and letters they sent home to their families and friends.

On July 16, 1942, the *Tribune* reported that Grimme had enlisted in the Army Air Corps and was transferred to Jefferson Barracks, Missouri. From there, Grimme undertook eighteen weeks of aviation training at Buckley Field in Denver, Colorado. A month and a half later, the September 2 *Tribune* carried a small article on page four reporting that the Grimme family had lent three of their sons — Malcolm, Leonard, and Verl — to the war effort. All three were still stateside.

Grimme's rank rose from private in July 1942, to staff sergeant in the spring of '43, and to tech sergeant in the fall of '44. By then, based in England, he was an Eighth Air Force Armament Specialist for B-24 Liberators, used in the bombing of Nazi warmaking installations. The Third Bombardment Division, of which Grimme was a member, was cited by President Franklin Roosevelt for its England-Africa shuttle bombing of Messerschmitt aircraft plants at Regensburg, Germany that August. Late that year, Grimme was promoted to master sergeant, the highest rank available to enlisted men in the Air Corps.

Grimme again set foot on Tipton County soil, when he came home July 5, 1945, for a thirty-day furlough following the end of the war. A July 6, 1945, *Tipton Tribune* article noted that brother Leonard had been home for a week, and brother Malcolm was due home "soon." Grimme was discharged from the Army in September.

His next life-changing moves took place in early 1946 when he joined with brother Paul to start their own business, Grimme Bros. Farm Supplies, and January 1947, when he married his sweetheart, Phyllis LaGarde.

After that, Grimme settled into a comfortable, yet active and productive life — husband, breadwinner, father to his and Phyllis' three children (Mike, Diane, and Sonita), community leader and volunteer, youth mentor, and Little League and basketball coach. His involvement with the kids earned him a rousing call-out by *Tribune* columnist R.D. Maney on February 7, 1951.

"A SALUTE to Verl Grimme!" Maney wrote. "If it has anything to do with boys ... he can be depended upon to offer his services any time. Many, many times, he does little things for the kids that you and I would overlook, and is a real favorite with the teenagers!

Coach Verl Grimme poses with the Hobbs Elementary School basketball team and cheerleaders after they won the 1948 "kids tournament." Pictured, front row from left, are: Eva Sue Bogue, Everett Stiner, Charles Jack, Larue Fecher, Betty Deverback; back row from left, are: Grimme, Paul Julius, Larry Clouser (who would later find Olene's body on a country road), Doyle Hobbs, and Darlene Overdorf.

He never hesitates ... one call is enough, and when the magic words, 'Would you help with the kids,' is sounded, he's right there, day or night!"

After his brother Paul was elected sheriff and sworn in on January 7, 1955, Grimme's community involvement took a giant leap forward. He became Paul's deputy, and for the next four years, his life was filled with challenges of all stripes, polka dots, and textures.

Even then, and throughout his years as sheriff, Grimme remained true to his tender spot for young people. Beryl Grimme recalls his brother Verl's practice of opening up a portion of the jail to kids in need — as he had for Tom Preston as a means of protecting him from Olene's angry father.

"He'd bring them in," Beryl said, "and they'd live in the jail on the second floor, which didn't have any bars, and they could come and go as they wanted. He had cots up there for them, and he'd keep them out of trouble.

"I saw him pull over more than one drunk kid and say, 'You just leave your car there, get in my car, and I'll take you home,'" Beryl recalled.

* * *

Verl Grimme was deputy sheriff under the tutelage of his big brother until 1958, when Paul lost his seat in the general election by just 97 votes to Clyde Overdorf. The new sheriff opted not to retain the former sheriff's younger brother as a deputy. That, however, wouldn't be the end of Overdorf's dealings with Verl.

Four years later, Grimme threw his brown, flat-brimmed deputy sheriff's hat into the ring, declaring himself a candidate for Tipton County sheriff. He easily won the primary, and went on to defeat Overdorf handily in the general election. In January 1963, he moved into the sheriff's residence at Madison and West Streets. His wife served as the jail matron. After completing his four years, Grimme won a second term on November 8, 1966 (his fifty-first birthday), once again dashing Overdorf's hopes. That time, Grimme defeated Overdorf by 1,406 votes, the second largest margin on the county ticket. When Grimme's eight-year stint as sheriff was up, he had built an impressive legacy that validated his innate leanings for altruism, compassion, and justice. Consequently, he had earned the respect of the community he served — save the Embertons' — as well as the officers with whom he had worked.

During his 2006 interview, Jim Pratt, who served the Tipton Police Department for twenty years and as chief from 1962 through 1972, spoke of his admiration for Grimme.

"I always got along with him," Pratt said. "He could be flighty, I guess. It didn't take too much to set him off once in a while. He would sometimes jump to a conclusion, but in the end, he usually got down to what he needed. He and his brother Paul were almost opposites."

Pratt explained that, while Paul was easygoing and enjoyed talking to just about anybody, Verl operated under a different tack.

"If Paul could find something out or get an answer, he would," Pratt recalled. "But Verl? He'd sometimes say, 'I don't want to talk to them.' Or, if somebody would ask him something, he'd say, 'Go find it out yourself.' That's just the way he was. But I never had trouble with Verl."

Beryl Grimme said essentially the same thing about his brother, Verl, but added that everyone who knew Verl considered him a good man, and some folks called him a hero.

Retired Tipton Police Officer Randy Horton had known Grimme well and admired him greatly. Horton got his start in law enforcement in the late 1960s and received most of his training from Grimme.

"Verl took me under his wing and taught me what it meant to be a law enforcement officer," Horton said during a 2017 interview.

"He was really dedicated to his job — really. You could tell he loved it. He worked hours like you would not believe and did it all. He knew what he was doing."

Horton recalled many good memories of Grimme. One story brought a chuckle.

"I loved riding with him," he said. "He liked to tell me he had some sort of gyroscope in his car because he could turn that curve out on [State Road] 28 at a hundred and ten miles an hour on the way to a wreck. We cleared [U.S. Highway] 31 with all four wheels and landed on the other side." Horton laughed again. "He was crazy. He wasn't afraid of nothing."

Horton recalled that one of the very first things he had noticed about Grimme was that he wore his gun on his left hip, even though he was right-handed. Horton demonstrated. "He wore his gun backwards," he said, swinging his right arm across his chest. "So he reached with his right hand to his left side — like Val Kilmer did in *Tombstone*."

Another time, Horton said, he saw Grimme threaten to shoot a man.

"The guy had beat the hell out of his wife," Horton explained. "When we pulled up, the guy was backing out of his driveway. Verl got out of the car and told him to 'open that door,' and the guy wouldn't do it. So Verl said, 'Open that door' again as he pulled out his gun and put it right up to the window. The guy got out. For a little guy, you've got to be like that."

Michael Colgate, who had worked for Grimme as a deputy before joining the Indiana State Police, admired Grimme's principles and integrity. Colgate wrote in a 2006 email that Grimme was "the kind of guy that would not cover up for even 'high-ranking businessmen.'"

"I had the pleasure of overhearing some rather heated exchanges between Verl and some of Tipton's so-called upper crust when they tried to interfere with him," Colgate continued. "When

I went to work for him as a deputy, he handed me a piece of folded paper and told me this was a list of the folks I could not arrest. When I opened it, the page was blank."

* * *

The conventional wisdom long held by members of the Tipton community insists that the Olene Emberton death investigation, under the leadership of Verl Grimme, was botched because he lacked the expertise and intellectual acuity.

"I always felt like it was a small town, and police didn't know how to handle a case like this," said Jennifer Cels.

"My dad was friends with Verl," Dixie Ihnat offered, "and I don't recall Dad ever saying Verl had told him anything at all about [Olene's case]. It was like he didn't want to discuss it or want anybody else interfering. … It was a small town, and I think [Verl] thought he was just going to pick up speeders. I think he was in over his head and didn't want to admit it."

Ann Reeves agreed, asserting, "They'd never had anything like that to deal with in this town."

In many ways, the Tipton of the 1950s and '60s was somewhat akin to the stereotypical idyllic, rural town — like those depicted in a Norman Rockwell painting or an old Disney movie — intimate, friendly, laidback, and bristling with neighborly spirit and goodwill. Certainly, Tipton was no Chicago or New York City, but neither was it insulated from human beings, whose darkest impulses occasionally drove them to commit odious deeds. In many ways, Tipton presented a strange, discombobulation of emergency situations that demanded the best of its police and sheriff's departments. Throughout the years that Verl Grimme worked for the sheriff's department, both as a deputy and as sheriff, he saw his share of emergencies ranging from everyday humdrum to bloodshed. Incidents included shoplifting, domestic abuse, wayward cyclists, curfew violators, bar fights, stray bullets, vending machine burglaries, vandals, Halloween tricksters, drunks, overturned trucks, sheep-killing dogs, missing hogs, trespassers, bad-check passers, stolen cars, speeders, high-speed chases, road rage, hit-and-runs, and traffic fatalities.

Besides all of that, he was clobbered by an arm bandaged in a plaster cast, forced to look for jewels pitched into a field following a Foster's Jewelry Store heist, investigated reports of a flying saucer, returned a "borrowed" toddler to its frantic mother, and worked a number of Tipton County homicides.

During his years as a deputy, Verl investigated two especially violent murders — Jack King, who was killed instantly on July 31, 1955, when his poker buddy ambushed him in a woods south of Tipton and shot him through the head; and Margaret Smith, a 45-year-old Tipton woman, fatally shot by an intruder on May 13, 1958, as she stood at her kitchen stove.

Although murders in Tipton County were anything but common during Grimme's service as deputy sheriff and sheriff, the on-the-job experience he gained should have afforded him more than enough expertise to properly conduct an investigation into the Olene Emberton case — at least to the extent the technology and forensics available in 1965 would permit. For example, rape kits were not available as an evidence-collection process until the late 1970s, and the first DNA-based conviction did not occur in the United States until 1987.

People who knew Verl Grimme agree that the Emberton case was his biggest disappointment. In that regard, his brother Beryl speculated, "I think he probably put out all the energy he could to solve it on account of she was a young girl. If it had been a young boy, it would have been the same thing."

Bob Zell agreed. "I think he wanted to solve it, just like all the rest of us did. We just ran out of leads, and there was no place to go with it."

Joe Watson was an attorney in Tipton for 58 years specializing in estate planning and real estate. The Embertons hired him in early 1966 to establish a trust fund for a $5,000 reward for information leading to the arrest of their daughter's murderer. Interviewed in November of 2016, Watson spoke highly of his good friend, Verl Grimme, and commented on how determined Grimme had been to discover what had happened to Olene and close the case.

"Verl thought he knew," Watson said, "but he couldn't prove it. He wouldn't tell me what he thought had happened; he wouldn't say who. He just had an opinion. It was all circumstantial evidence."

Randy Horton believed Grimme did everything possible to close the case.

"He felt like he had it solved," Horton recalled, although Grimme never shared his conclusion with him. "Why he gave up, I don't know."

When asked if Grimme perhaps had nowhere else to go due to a lack of evidence, Horton shook his head and shrugged.

"He got aggravated with the system," Horton said, "and the rumors. They were idiotic." •

> *"At first, I believed the rumors ...*
> *But I have learned that sometimes*
> *it is the person you least suspect."*
> — Floetta Scelta

14
RUMOR MILL

While many in the Tipton community believed the Tipton County Sheriff was out of his league dealing with the Emberton case, others were certain the truth was simply being covered up.

As with a number of high profile, historic cases — Jack the Ripper, the Black Dahlia, Lizzie Borden, Dr. Sam Sheppard among them — when clues fail to congeal in a logical explanation, conspiracies abound. The Emberton case was no exception.

Beginning as early as October 21, 1965, the unsubstantiated speculation and the excessive number of unfounded rumors seeping into the case were being mentioned in news reports. Rumbles of gossip only grew louder as the days passed.

The flow of false, inaccurate, and misleading information was disconcerting to Grimme and others on the case. Coroner Mitchell, for example, told the *Tipton Tribune* on October 28 that he repeatedly had been told stories "alleging facts which have never been made available to him." In the same article, Grimme, too, commented on the growing amount of gossip, grumbling that it was hampering the investigation.

The *Tribune*'s "Round Town and the Clock" columnist R.D. Maney also addressed the rumors that day. His piece, titled "STOP THE GOSSIP," read:

"We call on the people of the community, as well as those of surrounding areas, to stop second-guessing — and at least wait until the report in the Emberton case is received from the pathologist.

"From different sources, we hear stories that would curl your hair! All the experts are taking a crack at the solution. Some of the things they are saying are outlandish! The *Tribune* promises you that we will do all in our power to supply you with the facts as they are given. There have been difficulties in securing news … why we do not know — but propose to find out. A rehash of an old statement was carried by an out-of-town paper yesterday; the same story as before — and the same errors! Keep faith — forget the gossip … and wait for facts!"

Officers were obliged to check out every lead, and yet the groundless tips only wasted valuable man-hours and resources.

In the absence of credible leads, a frenzy of malicious conspiracy theories, some of them blatantly slanderous, went viral. Tales involving an unidentified drifter and a flasher provided colorful fodder for the imaginatively challenged, while other folks were spreading manure manufactured closer to home. One of those stories concerned an alleged secret organization of gay businessmen (all of them posing as happily married family men). Former Tipton Police Chief Jim Pratt had heard that story.

"That was a rumor two or three days after [Olene] disappeared," Pratt said during his 2006 interview. "There was a prominent lawyer here in town that supposedly had picked her up. And I guess the sheriff talked to him and said there wasn't anything to it. And one time, there was a story going around that a policeman had picked her up, and they didn't get anyplace on that either."

While the far-fetched, uncorroborated stories of high-profile men in the community gave the gossip hounds a tasty bone to chew, a few Tipton people chose to believe hearsay that was unabashedly poisonous.

One of those stories placed the blame on a member of the Emberton family, while another rumor claimed Floyd had profited from his daughter's death, possibly in the form of hush money accepted from the guilty party. As "proof" of the ill-gotten financial gain, they claimed Floyd had used it to bankroll two new businesses — the Emberton Trailer Court and Emberton Used Car Lot.

Obviously, those spreading the "personal gain" theory were unaware that Floyd had established both businesses long before Olene's death, as evidenced by the dates of the advertisements appearing in the *Tipton Tribune*.

Promoting his new trailer court, a display ad on page three of the June 10, 1963, *Tribune* reads:

ANNOUNCING
OPENING
NEW
TRAILER
COURT
IN TIPTON
Located
300 Block on
Sweetland Ave.
FLOYD
EMBERTON
PHONE OS 5-6859

Two years later, and exactly three months before Olene's disappearance, the earliest reference to Floyd's car lot appeared on the *Tribune*'s July 16, 1965, classified page. The ad reads:

FOR SALE — 62 Chevy $995 and other good used cars
Emberton's Used Car Lot, 336 Sweetland

Clearly, if common sense weren't enough to dispel the unfounded allegation that Floyd had profited financially from the death of his daughter, the ads should stand as indisputable proof that the rumors were without merit.

According to former Indiana State Police Officer Robert Zell, Floyd was aware that people in the community and even members of law enforcement had started looking at him as a possible suspect. After a while, the barrage of whispers and averted, sideways glances by his neighbors was more than he could stand. He finally relented to Grimme's requests that he and oldest son, Floyd Wayne, do what was necessary to conclusively confirm or erase the growing suspicions.

"The easiest way to do it was run a lie detector test," Zell said, "and if it proves negative on everything, okay, we can move on from that. If they didn't beat her up or do something to her — which we were pretty sure they didn't — but in order to make it positive, give them a lie detector test."

A November 26, 1965, *Tipton Tribune* story mentioned that "Mrs. Emberton informed the *Tribune* that the Sheriff's Department, in cooperation with State Police, had administered lie detector tests to both her husband and her son Floyd Jr.," the paper stated, "and that a test had been offered to another young man who, on the advice of his attorney, refused to take the test."

Although the story made no reference to the identity of the other young man, it did quote Grimme confirming, "that some tests had been given," and additional tests may yet be performed.

A January 12, 1966, *Tipton Tribune* article quoted Grimme about the rapidly churning rumor mill — the rumor *du jour* being that a solution to the Emberton case was forthcoming.

"Where these rumors spring from, I don't know," Grimme said. "Every one of the rumors I've heard has been repeated time and again, but apparently there are still a few pairs of ears they haven't reached, and when they do, the stories are given a new birth with absolutely no foundation."

Frustrated, Grimme emphasized that he followed through on them all.

"Every new rumor, some of them malicious and actually subject to slander charges, results in suspects," he said. "We check them all — some of them we've checked out half a dozen times on the chance there may be something we've missed. Everything has checked out negative. All I can tell the *Tribune* now is that there is no foundation for any new rumor. There are no arrests, no clues — I wish there were. I wish I had any kind of a lead, but I don't."

* * *

Despite Grimme's assurances, the rumors persisted. As the weeks and months rolled by with no charges filed, no suspects named, not even a clue revealed, gossip supplied the only answers the community could cling to. Throughout the intervening fifty-plus years since Olene Emberton's death, when Tipton residents get together and talk about the case, the rumors still fuel many of their narratives about what *really* happened.

Such discussions — in group settings and via email — occurred in early 2017 among members of Olene's high school class, and nearly everyone had heard one or more of the rumors, and some said they accepted the rumors as fact.

"There were so many rumors that floated around the town concerning Olene's death," wrote Vickie Porter. "Even to this day, I would not repeat any of them as obviously they could not have been true or there would have been evidence to support them and perhaps an arrest. … Without any facts, just rumor, it is hard to conclude if her death was intentional or accidental. When I think of Olene now, I still wonder, "What happened?"

"I always heard it was a businessman," said Ann Reeves.

"People were saying that it might have been some businessman in town," Terry Conwell said, echoing Reeves.

"I heard it *wasn't* a businessman," said Wanda Abney, dismissing the foregoing theory, "but a doctor."

"At first, I believed the rumors that some big shot in town did it and had it covered up," said Floetta Scelta. "But I have learned that sometimes it is the person you least suspect."

No one knew who did it, but some who bought into Scelta's person-least-suspected theory used it to stir up even more unsavory speculation, alleging that a loved one was responsible for Olene's death.

"We saw all this stuff in the paper," said life-long Tipton resident Anna Gipson, "that she was placed there and her clothes were folded. So I think whoever did that knew her and cared about her."

Gail Wix said the steady flow of gossip made her angry.

"Nobody did anything to find out what happened," she said. "It sounds like something was being hidden to protect someone's name."

Following that line of thought, Karyn Roseberry added, "It was very clear from every rumor I heard, there was a cover up."

With a sigh, Dixie Ihnat picked up the conversation. "That's the beauty of a small town. Everybody has a theory." Looking around the room at her former classmates, she said, "You tell you, and you tell you, and you tell you…"

However, according to another line of hearsay, the killer may have been a stranger who had been seen lurking about. Jill Edgar recalled the story told to her by Mary Edwards, the mother of Edgar's best school friend, Trina Edwards.

"Mary told me that a new man hanging around town was found to have pictures of Olene and, of course, Trina, on a wall in his apartment," Edgar wrote in a 2016 email. "But even as a kid green around the ears, I knew Mary to be a little imaginative where her daughter was concerned."

But of all the baseless, mean-spirited rumors, most cruel was the unconscionable story that shrugged off Olene's death as just desserts for her alleged promiscuity.

The haughty, judgmental pronouncement that Olene was in some way responsible for her awful fate has circulated for years. Blaming the victim — for example, "The victim was attacked because she was out too late, or in the wrong place, or dressed too provocatively..." — is a universally practiced, timeless tactic that shifts the responsibility for sexually violent crimes onto the injured person to make others feel superior and safe.

In a 2010 email, Neal Curry addressed the rumors that claimed Olene's fate was a consequence of her behavior. He wrote:

> "What ticks me off the most was the town just started to blame Olene for what happened. They started rumors about her that ranged from having affairs with half the businessmen in town to being the town tramp. They seemed to believe the worst in her before they would accept that Tipton had a murderer in its midst. Now they just don't talk about it anymore. No outrage, no calls for final justice. No anything. When Mrs. Emberton is gone, that will be the final nail in Olene's casket.
>
> "The Embertons were just a great family. I don't know why all this happened. Tipton society tried to paint Olene as a girl with moral problems, and this just infuriated me. I told Grimme this was just small town B.S. She was a good kid who never had a chance."

Like Neal Curry, Karyn Roseberry never bought into the blame-the-victim scenario.

"I think it was more the opposite," Roseberry declared. "I think Olene was more of a prude."

Jim Pratt was asked what he knew of Olene's relationship with Tom Preston. Pratt said Olene's girlfriends had confided to him that Preston was the only boy she had ever been intimate with.

Former State Police Officer Bob Zell said he had heard the same story from Olene's acquaintances. They also told him, he said, that she went along with it only because Preston wanted to.

Another baseless rumor that has persisted for decades alleges that Grimme participated in a conspiracy by hiding all the records related to it.

It's a fact that Grimme's case files have never been located, and many Tipton folks continue to insist he purposely destroyed them to protect the guilty parties. However, other people who have followed the case, especially those with law enforcement experience, have argued that the unfounded theory that Grimme destroyed the old case files is as easily discredited as the stories of the alleged suspects.

"I don't have any idea where those old files went to," Pratt said. "When Grimme left office, evidently a lot of paperwork left with him. … He might have written it down on a tablet, and it'd stay on his desk for a week. And finally he'd come in and he'd read it, [and say] 'Well, I'd better keep this,' and stick it back in a drawer someplace."

Bob Zell also addressed the question of the missing files. He suggested the loss might have been due to sloppy recordkeeping, which was common in the 1960s before small-town law enforcement agencies adopted modernized data storage systems. As sheriff, Grimme had the discretion of keeping track of his cases in any manner he chose, he said. When Grimme left office, he could have pitched whatever notes and paperwork he'd recorded, or he could have taken everything home and never given it another thought.

"At that time," Zell said, "whenever a sheriff left office, he either took his files with him or he destroyed them. There were no continual files. I know [newly elected sheriffs] used to complain about that. They'd take office and wouldn't have a thing. No continuity from one administration to the next."

Former State Police Officer Michael Colgate, who was well acquainted with Grimme, expressed a similar opinion about the once common file-keeping habits of local sheriffs.

"Case reports as we now know them were non-existent at that time in the Tipton County Sheriff's Office," Colgate wrote in his 2006 letter. "At least I never made or saw one made. Any notes taken by an officer were simply kept by that officer with most information being passed on by word of mouth."

* * *

The December 3, 1965, *Kokomo Tribune* carried a page one retrospective on the Emberton case from Floyd and Roxie's point of view. They talked longingly of their daughter and about her last day of life, in particular. They also spoke of their dismay with the investigation, not understanding how, in a small town like Tipton, it was possible that no one knew how their daughter had died or who had abandoned her body along that country road.

The *Kokomo Tribune* stated that the Emberton family had their own ideas about what had happened, but nothing solid, "just small clues and bits of information." They firmly believed their daughter had gotten into a car with someone familiar to her, someone she trusted, the paper wrote.

The story went on, quoting Roxie. "[Olene] didn't have many dates and went around with a small group of people," she said. "I think that if teenagers are involved in this, adults are helping them cover it up."

"There is someone in this town who knows what happened that night," Floyd told the *Tribune*. "I told the sheriff we weren't going to let this die."

Dave Berkemeier, who moved to the Tipton community from Rushville in 1981, served as Tipton mayor from 1992 through 1999. In early 2017, he recounted a conversation he'd had with Roxie Emberton early in his first term.

"She told me nobody would listen to her," Berkemeier said, "so I told her I would listen. I invited her into my office and after a few minutes, she began to talk about her daughter. She told me she thought that before Olene had been killed, some of the local businessmen had taken advantage of her."

According to Berkemeier, at the time of that conversation, Roxie believed the rumors about the businessmen to be true. However, in later years, according to her daughter-in-law, Debbie, Roxie dismissed the old rumors about the businessmen as bunk and was certain about who was responsible for her daughter's death. •

> "*He wanted attention. That's all he wanted.*"
> — Jo Anna Powell

15
WHO WAS TOM PRESTON?

Roxie may have eventually figured out who had watched her daughter die, but initially, she and Floyd blamed Olene's former boyfriend, Tom Preston, who ironically would become the second member of the T.H.S. Class of '66 to die.

Although some of Olene's classmates recalled Preston as the great love of her brief life, she shared him with many other girls from Tipton High and neighboring schools. Thanks to the trail of broken hearts Preston left behind, the tall, good-looking, proverbial bad boy with bleached-blond hair and a wily sneer had attained legendary status long before he met Olene. Had he only known that dating Olene would cement his legend in ways no one could have imagined, he might have steered clear of her. Regrettably, that wasn't the case, and Preston went on doing what came naturally.

One of his closest high school buddies, Bill Brackney, spoke on the record in August of 2006 about his old friend.

"I can't tell you how many girls have told me that Tom gave them their first kiss," Brackney said.

Asked if the two had ever talked about Preston being a suspect, Brackney replied, "No, we didn't have to."

According to Brackney and another of Preston's close buddies,

Ed Achenbach, Olene's death tore Preston apart, not only because he'd lost a friend in such a terrible, shocking manner, but because he was one of the first people that Olene's family and local law enforcement looked at as a suspect. It was a distinction Preston was never able to shake, Achenbach said, and it likely contributed to the acceleration of his self-destructive behavior during the final months of his life.

The day after Olene was found, several papers reported that, while no arrests had yet been made, two boys had been held Sunday and Monday nights at the Tipton County jail in protective custody. Angry threats made by Floyd Emberton had made it necessary to lodge the boys temporarily at the jail. The October 20, 1965, *Indianapolis News* identified one of the boys as Preston.

In a 2005 telephone interview, former Tipton High School Principal Charles Edwards recalled Floyd Emberton's temper.

"The Embertons had such a tough time," Edwards said. "During that time, [the sheriff] kept Tom Preston at the jail for safety, and we locked the school. Mr. Emberton was belligerent, and he said he was going to get him."

Floyd Emberton never did "get him," but Preston's friends said the threat weighed heavily on his psyche.

So certain had Floyd been of Preston's guilt that several weeks after Olene's death, he parked his daughter's bright red Chevy across the street from the Preston home in the two hundred block of West Madison Street and left it there for a solid month. It apparently was a tactic intended to wear Preston down and goad him into confessing. Floyd's scheme proved fruitless, however, and the car eventually disappeared from West Madison Street.

Preston's friends, unlike Olene's father, knew murder was not a part of his makeup.

"Tom could be one of the sweetest, kindest, most considerate guys in the world," said Gail Wix, who had dated Preston off and on during her junior and senior years of high school.

Wix's first date with Preston illustrates the sweeter side of his personality.

"The first car date I had with Tom," Wix recalls fondly, "he only had a driver's permit. So when he arrived to pick me up, his mother was in the car. She had to be next to him while he drove us to the Diana Theatre. Tom was behind the wheel, his mother was beside him, and I was riding shotgun. Thank goodness the car didn't have bucket seats, or I would have been in the back!"

Pausing, she quickly added, "That's the part I loved. But he could also be rude and obnoxious, mostly when he was drinking."

Tom Preston's high school graduation photo.

According to Neal Curry, who regarded Preston as his best friend, Floyd Emberton always disliked Preston.

"Most fathers did," Curry wrote in his 2010 email. "Tom had 'that look' fathers disliked. Tom thought it was funny."

Expressing his obvious affection for his good friend, in 2017 Curry wrote:

> "Tom was the single most girl hound I believe I ever knew. He was a junior high lounge lizard, if ever there was one. He always was looking for girls, no matter what.
>
> "Tom was the first person I knew who regularly used peroxide on his hair. Most people thought he was blond, but he had reddish brown hair that he washed with peroxide then went out in the sun. Like I said, always the lothario.

"His home life could be rough. His mother was constantly in a foul mood. ... Tom's dad was a likeable character who had the gift of gab — typical salesman of the time. His dad was always gone, and I believe they [his parents] preferred it that way.

"Tom adored his dad and always tried to be like him. He even bought the same shoes his dad wore. [His dad] smoked Mersham pipes, and Tom would always show people the collection he had. Tom even tried smoking one himself at times.

"Everybody had to tiptoe around his mom, and when his dad was home, he would drink and the arguments would come. Tom was planning to go to college in Florida to get as far away from home as possible. Tom had an alcohol problem really early in life, and I can only guess he was copying Dad."

Alcohol was the culprit behind Preston's tragic death in 1966. In Curry's 2010 email, he reflected on the painful memory of his friend's death and admitted to a degree of guilt that still ate at him. He wrote:

"Tom snapped his neck. There wasn't even a bruise on him. He hit the dash just hard enough to do damage — no seat belts in that old car. Tom had snuck into my car and taken a bottle of bourbon I had under the seat and was drinking when it happened. I felt like if it hadn't been there, [the wreck] might not have happened. Tom was drinking all the time by then, and you just wonder if things could have been different."

Few people knew, according to Curry, that Preston had been admitted to college in Florida. Had he survived the car crash, he would have entered college that fall as a freshman.

Curry said it took a long time for him to "get over" both Tom Preston's and Olene Emberton's deaths.

"I always felt that they never had a chance to start," he wrote.

Some of Preston's classmates thought they knew him relatively well, many remembering him as a "bad boy." But Sandy Lewis dismissed that assessment, arguing, "He wasn't a bad boy. That wasn't him. That was the persona he wanted to give off."

Sharon Foland agreed. "I never considered him a bad boy. I remember him for being outgoing."

Another of Olene's classmates, Mary Coan, commented on various aspects of the Emberton case.

"When I learned [Olene] had been found dead," she wrote in her 2017 email, "I was terrified at first. Was there a killer on the loose? I never believed Tom Preston did it. There were so many rumors. I felt bad for him and his family."

Reminded of the way Olene's body had been placed alongside that country road, Ann Reeves immediately defended Preston's integrity.

"He might have been a little wild … but I never thought Tom was capable of anything like that."

Marijane Jay concurred. "I can't picture Tom being that aggressive."

"We couldn't imagine *anyone* being that aggressive," added Dixie Ihnat.

Two other old friends, Jennifer Cels and Terry Conwell, agreed that Preston was basically a likeable, good boy with an overt tendency toward mischief making.

"I always liked Tom," Cels said. "I thought he'd be getting into trouble his whole life. He wasn't a bully, just mischievous."

When asked to speculate on who might have left Olene's body on that country road, Conwell said, "I sure didn't think it was Tom. I know he was a little on the wild side sometimes, but I couldn't picture him [harming Olene]. I couldn't imagine any teen doing that."

Vickie Porter recalled first meeting Preston when he and his family moved to Tipton from Florida in the late 1950s.

"He lived a block behind my classmate and friend Jo Anna Weber [Powell]," Porter wrote. "Tom was all boy, mischievous, but I never found him to display a violent nature. I liked Tom and considered him a grade school friend. I was not close to Tom in high school, but I knew he was dating Olene. I could never imagine Tom doing anything so violent as to kill someone."

Classmate Randy Horton said he didn't run with Preston, but he knew him well.

"Tom seemed like a normal, everyday guy to me," Horton said.

Jill Edgar and Preston had shared a few of the same friends, some of whom were her girlfriends, who had dated him.

"He was a cute boy who had a wild side to him," Edgar said.

Ann Reeves was reminded that Preston's former relationship with Olene had caused many in the community to look at him differently after her death and to wonder if he had been the one responsible.

"[Some] people thought that when Tom passed away he'd gotten his 'just reward,' or that it was karma," she said, slowly shaking her head. "They even mentioned how weird it was that he died on the curve around Hobbs, near the same area they'd found Olene. But I knew Tom. He was like a puppy dog after Olene. They were like two *love nuts*."

Shirley Huss' and Jo Anna Powell's take on Preston was less sentimental.

"Tom was rowdy," Huss proclaimed. "I worked at Carter's [grocery store] with him, and after it closed, he'd go into the back of the meat case and swallow oysters and bring them back up."

Powell jumped in to give context to the questionable behavior Huss had characterized.

"He wanted attention," Powell said. "That's all he wanted."

Powell noted that she had known Preston before high school, when they were elementary and junior high school students at St. John's Catholic School. St. John's was rife with disciplinary challenges for Preston, because, as Powell noted, there was virtually no tolerance for horseplay.

"Tom would get in trouble," she said, "and the priest would give him a whipping with a Ping-Pong paddle. I always felt like he just wanted someone to pay attention."

Perhaps it was Floetta Scelta's poignant memories that painted the most sympathetic portrait of Preston. She wrote:

> "Tom Preston — one guy I really wasn't fond of. He had a sarcastic attitude and was one of the guys who I would never have gone out with. Not that he would have ever asked. We were friends [and] had gone out 'running around' with a group a few times. A few nights before he was killed, I saw him, and he asked me to ride around with him. I told him I would.
>
> "Tom talked about Olene and said he did not kill her. He cried and said he would never have a chance in this town because of all the things her dad was doing — parking her car in front of the Prestons' house, etc. [Her father] knew she liked [Preston], and he may have taken advantage of that. But I don't believe he killed her."

* * *

According to former State Police Officer Robert Zell and former Tipton Police Chief James Pratt, the police and sheriff's departments had looked seriously at only two suspects. One was Preston because of his relationship with Olene. He was the state police detectives' number one suspect, Zell said. While neither he nor Pratt could recall who the other suspect had been, Zell was adamant that Preston was the officers' primary person of interest.

Zell explained:

> "He [Preston] was the one we were all sort of zeroing in on. We had questioned him once or twice and didn't have enough to hold him, and we let him go. In fact, we weren't sure he had really committed a crime. We wanted him to tell us if he was the guy who was with her when she died, but we never got to that point.
>
> "Of course, when we found her car over here on Green Street, there was no sign of anything in disarray, or a scuffle or anything around the car. We canvassed the neighborhood. Nobody heard or saw anything. They just got up one day and saw that car sitting out there. So it appeared to us that whoever she went with, she went willingly. Whether it was Preston or not, we don't know. We suspected that it was, but we couldn't prove that. I guess that's the reason the whole thing just sort of died on the vine, because we ran out of any place to go with it. ... About every name that her friends threw out at us, we questioned. But we didn't have any place to go. I'm sure we picked up on the fact that she had this ex-boyfriend, [and] that she had broken it off, but he didn't want to break up."

* * *

Tom Preston was eighteen years old, when he lost his life shortly before midnight on Thursday, June 8, 1966, in a car crash in eastern Tipton County. The Tipton community learned of Preston's death the next morning, when they opened their *Kokomo Morning Times*. The paper carried a brief story on its front page under the headline, "Tipton Lad Dies in Crash."

Preston had been the passenger of a speeding car headed east along State Road 28. As the vehicle approached the curve at Hobbs, the driver lost control.

"The car slid broadside, rolled over into the ditch and wrapped itself around a tree," the paper reported.

Pratt was called to the scene of the fatal crash, where he found the car on its side. Inside the car, Preston was lying on top of the other boy, who begged Pratt, "Get him off me. He's crushing me to death."

"We finally got the car upright and got them out.," Pratt said.

Amazingly, none of the driver's injuries was life threatening. Preston, conversely, died instantly when he was thrown head first into the car's dashboard, breaking his neck. He also had suffered a broken arm and a broken back.

Preston's funeral was held the following Saturday morning at St. John's Catholic Church. Officiating was Father Jerome Walski, the same priest, who years earlier had introduced Preston to his Ping-Pong paddle. Preston is buried in Tipton's Fairview Cemetery. •

16
AUTHOR'S POINT OF VIEW: THE TOM PRESTON I REMEMBER

I've often joked that Tom Preston was my first sociopath — a reference to his seemingly oblivious disregard for the sensitivities of his squeeze *du jour*. I think I qualified as such a time or two. He was, after all, my first date, my first aborted kiss, and my first consummated kiss. But I'm getting ahead of myself.

I confess that throughout my first three years of high school, I had a little crush on him. It wasn't serious, and knowing I was just one of many girls vying for his attention, I had no expectations. But one benefit I did receive during our friendship was a sobering glimpse into the psyche of a troubled, scared young man who concealed his demons behind a façade of cool defiance.

Tom always tended to thumb his nose at rules that didn't suit him. While such behavior likely irritated his rule-abiding classmates, a great number of his peers envied his rambunctious, rebellious conduct. It was part of his appeal.

Even now, I can still easily conjure up the image of the fair-complected teenaged boy with the sharp, finely chiseled features, piercing green eyes, and bleached-blond hair. I still picture him in those peg-legged pants that had become so popular in the mid 1960s, with the tail of his white Oxford shirt untucked and the sleeves rolled up to his elbows. I remember the swoosh of his Thom McAn penny loafers brushing across the tile floor as he sauntered down the school's long, dark hallways exuding a confidence that probably wasn't really there. I can also hear his signature catcall — that drawn-out, deep-throated "*Whoooop*," which he grunted like an Elvis wannabe for the benefit of each passing cutie who met his gaze.

And yet, when circumstances required a less scintillating persona, such as meeting my parents or conversing with Tipton High School Principal Charles Edwards, he could instantly transform into the deferential boy next door. More than once, I saw him change from a freewheeling Jim Stark (James Dean's character in *Rebel Without a Cause*) to a straight-laced, kiss-up Eddie Haskell (of *Leave it to Beaver* fame) without a lick of apparent effort.

In retrospect, however, it's obvious that as Tom's need to bolster his defenses escalated, his B.S. congealed ever tighter. Accordingly, he wouldn't hesitate to start flinging it for sport, like a Frisbee of misdirection whenever necessary.

Even more telling and concerning was his increasing use of alcohol and his recklessness. Back then, I wasn't worldly enough to comprehend the motivations behind Tom's destructive behavior. In fact, I have long worried that because I bought into his exciting, edgy, and fearless demeanor, I had inadvertently encouraged it, thus making me complicit in his ill-fated journey.

Before St. John's Catholic School permanently closed at the end of the 2014 school year, its students attended grades one through eight there and then transferred to public high school. Tom was a St. John's kid and, even as small as Tipton was (and still is), I have no recollection of him until we entered high school in 1962.

During the second semester of our freshman year, he sat directly behind me in Ken Shoup's health class. Tom sat in the last desk in our row, making it difficult for Mr. Shoup's keen eyes to catch all his antics. And they were abundant. Tom was forever taunting and teasing all the girls around him, but he chose to inflict the brunt of his "playfulness" on me. Of all his pranks, the most alarming involved a switchblade knife.

For the record, in those days, Tipton had no rules against bringing weapons to school. While I don't recall anyone bringing firearms, pocketknives were quite common. A pocketknife was considered a convenience, a tool with many useful applications, such as turning screws, peeling apples, and prying tops off pop bottles. In Tom's case, however, he had one purpose in wielding that pocketknife in Mr. Shoup's classroom, and that was to continually poke me in the back with the sharp tip of its blade. He thought

I snapped this picture of Tom at a party at the home of Gail Perdue (now Wix) on a Saturday night during the winter of 1965. Standing is Jimmy Henderson, Class of '65.

it was hilarious. I'm almost embarrassed to admit that, despite my whispered protests, I did too.

After enduring his torment for the entire semester, I conspired with my friend Karyn Harkness (now Roseberry) to meet Tom and his friend, Jerry Howard, the first Saturday night of our summer vacation. Karyn and I walked uptown, where we met our waiting dates under the marquee of the Diana Theatre.

We each forked over our sixty cents at the ticket booth, and the boys ushered us girls to our seats in the theater's back row, directly below the clock. *Uh-oh*, I thought. The seats were in the heart of the legendary make-out section. I was nervous enough without the pressure of *that*. But, as it turned out, there was no need to worry. Yet. The lights had barely dimmed, when Tom suggested we blow the movie and take a walk. So the four of us filed out of the theater and strolled the six blocks to the park.

Once there, Karyn and Jerry headed toward the playground for their own adventures, while Tom and I climbed into the officials' box overlooking the Little League baseball diamond to "talk," and that's exactly what we did. The topics we discussed involved school, summer break, vacations, and friends, but as the sky grew darker and the stars began to sparkle, something shifted. My nerves settled down, and I think, for a little while, Tom and I connected as friends. I can't remember why that sweet moment ended, but when it did, Tom abruptly returned to his comfort zone — his bad-boy persona. That's when he swooped in to plant a kiss. I, being the shy, self-conscious greenhorn, did what came naturally and ducked, introducing his pucker to the back of my head.

I never had another formal date with Tom, but because we shared the same circle of friends, our paths crisscrossed regularly until his death. During those years, we shared a few moments that, even now, make me smile in a wistful kind of way.

Behind one of those smiles is the memory of that first consummated kiss I mentioned in the first paragraph of this chapter. That particular moment stands out because the kiss was delivered during a game of spin the bottle in full view of several of my friends who had gathered in my kitchen for an impromptu party, while my parents sat watching TV in the next room, not twenty feet away.

Some would say Tom Preston was not a nice guy. Although I'd like to differ, I can't because his behavior often demonstrated a destructive tendency toward others, as well as to himself. I'm not referring to his mischievous, childish pranks — like hiding in the shadows and throwing eggs at my car as I drove by, or tying an inflated condom to the antenna of his neighbor's car. While such shenanigans may have been annoying for their target, the misbehavior was harmless and a little amusing. What wasn't harmless or amusing was sneaking onto the farm of his mentally challenged classmate and chopping off the tail of the boy's cherished horse. Nor was it amusing when, in a drunken stupor, he opened the passenger door of his friend's speeding car and threatened to throw himself onto the highway. Or trying to have his way with God knows how many young women.

Prior to our senior year, I spent the summer visiting relatives in Southern California. My good friend, Wanda Cherry (now Abney), planned a going-away party for me the night before I left town, and Tom showed up. After about an hour, Tom and another boy got into an argument over something stupid. Tom called the boy a "son of a bitch," and before we knew it, Tom was holding his bloody front teeth in his hand.

One year later, he was dead.

I've never forgotten the morning I learned he had died. My mom rushed into my room, shaking the front page of the *Kokomo Morning Times* in my face, startling me into consciousness. "Tom Preston was killed in a car wreck," she gasped, her tone revealing an emotion I couldn't recognize — the actualization of a mother's worst fear.

What she had said was too much for me to absorb. I knew Tom wasn't dead. I was positive she was mistaken. I took the paper and read the story. I didn't know what to say. Or do. Or feel.

Since then, I've wondered countless times what course Tom's life might have taken had he not died in that crash. What kind of man might he have become? What triumphs and joys might he have experienced? How many lives might he have touched — for better or for worse? After pondering those questions, I'm always hopeful he would have straightened out his life and found happiness.

One question I don't have to ponder, however, is whether Tom had been the one who discarded Olene's body alongside that desolate road. •

Tom Preston's grave marker in Fairview Cemetery, Tipton

> *"This is my home, and no one wants a solution to the case more than I do."*
> — Sheriff Verl Grimme

17
PINKERTON TO THE RESCUE

The Embertons' faith in Grimme had been waning even before he announced the failure of the pathologist and the toxicologist to determine why Olene died. Floyd and Roxie, like a growing number of anxious doubters clamoring for answers, had reached a conclusion about the sheriff: He was out of his depth.

That belief, bolstered by Grimme's failure to make an arrest, prompted the Embertons to accept help from Floyd's employer, Steel Parts, and its union.

On November 23, 1965, the *Tipton Tribune* announced that members of Local 3875 of the United Steelworkers had raised money to help the Embertons retain the services of the Pinkerton Detective Agency, renowned since the days of Jesse James and the Dalton Gang. Floyd, who was a member of the local and a fifteen-year Steel Parts employee, also had contributed an undisclosed amount to the fund.

The November 24 *Kokomo Morning Times* also carried the story, revealing that the members of the union local took a vote and agreed to give $500 to the investigation. The story revealed that the Pinkerton services were pricey — $7 per hour plus expenses for each detective. "Therefore," as the story noted, "the original $500 donation made by the Steelworkers Union headed by Garland Maddox, who thought of the idea, must be supplemented by other funds if it is necessary to continue the investigation for very long."

In addition, Ted Morris and Don Essig, officers of Farmers Loan & Trust in Tipton, volunteered to solicit additional donations from the community to help pay the Pinkerton agency.

Maddox said he and his fellow union members felt that Olene's death had touched the entire community. Thus, he urged everyone to help find the answers, and possibly her killer, by making a donation.

Grimme told the *Tipton Tribune* that he welcomed the Pinkerton agency and other investigators, private as well as public, that might help him find new evidence. He also said he would be glad to share all the information he had uncovered with the agency's detectives. Additionally, Tipton County Prosecutor Richard Regnier promised to provide any assistance the private investigators might need.

What could a Pinkerton detective do that a team of trained law enforcement officers couldn't? The question was put to former Howard County Sheriff Marty Talbert during his February 2018 interview. He explained:

> "I think a lot of times people hire those folks for peace of mind to continue working on the case. Private investigators also have a different leeway. For example, police have to read them their rights, and P.I.'s don't have to operate in that same manner. I think it's just keeping the investigation active, having a different set of eyes. There are cases where P.I.'s have continued to dig and solved a case after law enforcement stopped due to a lack of leads."

* * *

Pinkerton's National Detective Agency is the oldest and arguably the best-known detective firm in American history. Founded in 1850 in Chicago by Allan Pinkerton, the firm originally specialized in protecting railroad shipments. Prior to the start of the Civil War, Allan Pinkerton uncovered a plot to assassinate President Abraham Lincoln, and from then until the end of the war, he served as head of the Union Intelligence Service, which later became the U.S. Secret Service. By 1870, Pinkerton and his men were going after outlaws who terrorized the West, including desperadoes such as Jesse James, the Dalton Brothers, and Butch Cassidy's gang. After Allan Pinkerton died in 1884, the agency stayed in the family for several generations. By 1960, the agency's headquarters had relocated to New York City, overseeing forty-five branch offices nationwide, which included one in Indianapolis. The Indianapolis branch at that time was housed in the historic Chamber of Commerce Building at 320 North Meridian Street. Today, Pinkerton's is part of Securitas AB, the world's largest provider of security services. It maintains an Indianapolis office in the Parkstone Office Center Building, located on the city's northwest side.

* * *

The same day the *Tipton Tribune* announced that the Embertons had retained the Pinkerton agency, the *Kokomo Tribune* made a different but equally intriguing announcement: It too was offering a $500 reward for information that would lead to a successful closure of the case.

Richard H. Blacklidge, then the *Kokomo Tribune*'s publisher, said the reward would go to the first private person who provided new information leading to the arrest and conviction of the individual responsible for Olene's death.

"We are deeply concerned that this should happen in our area," Blacklidge said, "and we hope that by offering the reward, we might help authorities solve the mystery."

The *Kokomo Tribune* contacted Roxie Emberton about the reward. She said it was "a fine idea." The paper took the opportunity to ask her to comment on the progress of the investigation. Roxie, as usual, didn't mince words.

"My daughter had too small a group of friends for this case not to have been solved," she said. "Olene was too good a girl to have to face death this way."

The Kokomo paper also asked Grimme what he thought about the reward.

"I welcome the reward to help bring out anyone that might know something," he said. "We have felt all along someone knows something, but they may not feel it is important information. We're not against anything that will help us find out what happened."

A November 26 *Tipton Tribune* story stated it had confirmed that "at least" forty-eight law enforcement officers from the city police, the county sheriff's office, and the Indiana State Police were still working the case, interrogating acquaintances and possible suspects and rechecking leads.

"This is my home," Grimme told the *Tribune*, "and no one wants a solution to the case more than I do. We're still getting occasional information and even if it checks out to nothing, we're following up every lead given to us."

* * *

By the time the announcement about the Pinkerton agency appeared in the Tipton and Kokomo papers, its agent, who identified himself on his reports only as "W.R.S.," was already on the case. The three reports he filed on Monday, November 29 show that he made his first run to Tipton at 9:00 a.m. on the preceding Tuesday (November 23), which was the same day the *Tipton Tribune* had run the story announcing the Embertons had retained the firm.

"I drove to Tipton, Indiana, and searched an area south and west of the town [of] Tipton in the area of the old Emberton farm," W.R.S. wrote. "No leads were developed."

He next reported that he had talked with Roxie, who gave him permission to search Olene's room and personal belongings. "This also met with negative results," W.R.S. wrote.

At Floyd's request, W.R.S. spoke with the owner of Rayl Auto Sales, Kokomo, who "offered no new leads and only repeated rumors and hearsay."

At noon, the agent met with Floyd and Roxie at the office of Tipton County Prosecutor Richard Regnier. They agreed that a contract would be written laying out the terms and payment for the Pinkerton services.

In the days following, W.R.S. returned to Tipton several times. On Wednesday, November 24, according to W.R.S.'s report, he contacted Sheriff Grimme, who told him, "…no new developments had occurred." He also wrote that Grimme had driven him "to the area[s] where the Emberton body was found and where Olene's car had been parked."

W.R.S. reported that he had spoken with three potential witnesses, none of whom could provide new information or leads. He then drove to the 400 block of North Green Street, where Olene's car had been found, and interviewed several of the area residents. Among them was Olene's classmate, Jennifer Wiggins (now Cels), who lived in the house just steps from where the vehicle had been parked.

During her February 2017 telephone interview, Cels recalled driving home from school that November day in 1965. She was headed north on Main Street, when she noticed a dark-colored sedan that she didn't recognize following directly behind her. Nor did she recognize the man behind the wheel or his passenger. She thought nothing of it, even when she turned west onto North Street and the sedan turned west too. She still gave no thought to the car, even when it turned north onto Green Street behind her. It wasn't until the unfamiliar automobile pulled into her driveway behind her that the red flags finally unfurled.

Cels threw open her car door and climbed out. The stranger, who likely was W.R.S., climbed out of his car, and that's when she got her first good look at him.

"He had on dress pants, a nice shirt, and a sports jacket," she said, "and he wore glasses. He wasn't that old. I'm going to say early thirties."

She didn't think he posed a threat, so she stepped toward him.

"We kids weren't scared of anything at that time of our lives," she said with a laugh. "Not a bit frightened. I walked right up to him, and there couldn't have been more than six or seven feet between us. … I didn't feel threatened. I was just oblivious."

The man introduced himself, explaining that he was with the Pinkerton Detective Agency. He asked if she minded answering a few questions about Olene Emberton. Cels told him she was happy to share all she knew, especially if it meant helping to solve the mystery.

"That's when the other guy got out of the car," she said, adding that both men appeared mild-mannered and displayed a professional, non-threatening demeanor. "My mother was home, but she didn't realize this was going on. Then they asked me their questions: 'What's your relationship to Olene?' … 'When was the last time you saw her?'"

What the detectives wanted most was information about Olene's car being parked in front of the Wigginses' home the night she disappeared.

Cels told them she couldn't remember what time she had gotten in that night, but she hadn't noticed the car until her mother, Mary Wiggins, had arrived home from work about 12:30 a.m. As her mother walked through the front door, Cels said, she commented that a car was parked in front of their house. That seemed unusual to them both. Cels recalled looking out the window but didn't recognize the car as Olene's until the next morning in the light of day.

"I thought it must have broken down," she said. "There was not a bit of concern in my head. But the car was still there when I came home later, and I wondered why. I remember going to school Monday morning thinking it odd that her car was still there. But after they held us in school and I didn't know why, then it was a little creepy. I never saw anyone around the car until after they found Olene's body. The police said they were going to leave the car there a few days, but I can't remember how long."

As it turned out, Cels said, she didn't feel she'd been very much help to the Pinkerton detective. "I didn't have much to tell him," she said, "but he jotted a few things down. He didn't stay long, maybe fifteen minutes. Then they left, and I never saw them again."

W.R.S. noted in his report of November 24 that he also spoke with Mary Wiggins and three other residents of the neighborhood without turning up a single new lead. His report states that he again spoke with the Embertons before calling it a day.

W.R.S. returned to Tipton on Friday, November 26 and met again with the county prosecutor. In his report, W.R.S. noted, "... spoke with Richard O. Regnier, who reviewed the entire case with us. Regnier also said the clothing examination had not as yet been completed by the state police and that no new information had been developed."

The report continued, "I familiarized V.D.M. [Vincent D. McGraw, then head of the Indianapolis-based Pinkerton office] with the area where the body was found and we searched the farm buildings north of this area." The report ended with a note about meeting with the sheriff: "Sheriff Grimme stated that he had not developed any new leads, so returned to Indianapolis."

Over the next seven weeks, W.R.S. filed eight more reports. The common thread connecting them all was Verl Grimme's recurrent, dismissive claim: "No new developments." Despite Grimme's cold shoulder, W.R.S recorded two developments that were significant. The notes appear on the Monday, December 6, 1965, report.

First, W.R.S. wrote that Grimme informed him that a polygraph had been administered to a friend of Tom Preston's and cleared Preston of any involvement in Olene's death.

W.R.S.'s second notation of consequence on the December 6 report is long and detailed, providing the only specifics available describing the crime scene. The notation had been recorded after W.R.S.'s meeting with Tipton County Coroner Chester Mitchell at his funeral home. Following is a summary of W.R.S.'s notes:

- [Mitchell] stated he was the coroner for Tipton County and that when he was called to the area where the Emberton body was found, already present were Sheriff Grimme, State Police detectives, two men from the Young-Nichols Funeral Home, and several others thought to be investigators from the area.
- The gravel road was measured thirty-one feet, six inches from fence to fence.
- Olene's head was against the east fence, and her left toe was four feet, seven inches from the gravel.
- Her right toe was four feet from the gravel, and the distance from her left toe to the right toe was four feet.
- She had a natural expression on her face, her eyes partially closed. There were no bruises, cuts, or torn flesh visible, but there were a few bloodstained blades of grass at the opening of her vagina.
- She wore only a gold necklace.
- Olene's clothing was stacked at her left shoulder with her panties partially draped across her face.
- The clothing was not examined before it was placed

Tipton County Sheriff Verl Grimme looks over the place where Olene Emberton's body was found, next to a field-access road north and west of Hobbs. Her head was lying next to the fence (1) with her clothes piled beside her (2) and her glasses near her feet (3). (Photo from the October 20, 1965, Kokomo Morning Times *and reprinted with permission of the* Kokomo Tribune.*)*

in plastic bags to be taken to the lab, but her skirt appeared to have been torn or cut.
- Her bra did not show signs of being pulled from her body; rather it had been taken off normally.
- The autopsy revealed that Olene had died between 12:30 and 4:30 a.m. Sunday, approximately twelve hours before her body was found. Even though Sunday and Monday were sunny with temperatures in the mid-eighties, her body was not bloated or sunburned. Thus the medical examiner and coroner assumed her body had been kept in a cool place overnight.
- It seemed unlikely that one man could have thrown her body the distance necessary.
- No tire tracks, footprints, or other evidence was found at the scene.
- No death report had as yet been filed because the prosecutor wanted to wait until a cause of death had been determined, although the autopsy did not reveal the cause.

The only other significant piece of information contained in the Pinkerton reports was recorded Friday, December 10. W.R.S. wrote simply, "I drove to Danville, Indiana, and by prior arrangements, I obtained a copy of the autopsy report submitted to Sheriff Grimme after examining Olene Emberton. Returned to Indianapolis and wrote this report."

W.R.S. had picked up the autopsy report in Danville at the Hendricks County Hospital, where Dr. James McFadden, the pathologist on Olene's case, headed up the hospital's laboratory and pathology departments. Unfortunately, the recipient of the autopsy report obtained by W.R.S. is unknown. Also unknown is what became of it. Grimme's copy disappeared as well.

When McFadden retired in 1984, his Physicians Clinical Lab of Lafayette closed, and its records were transferred to Home Hospital, also in Lafayette. When Home Hospital closed in 2010, its medical records were sent to St. Elizabeth Hospital, also in that city. However, records more than ten years old were destroyed. Because the Indiana State Police had investigated the Emberton case, it seems that the pathologist's official report of Olene's autopsy should be safely stored in her case file at the state police office in Pendleton or the headquarters in Indianapolis. Inexplicably, it is not.

W.R.S. wrote his next report on December 15 and filed it December 28. In it, he stated:

> "We drove to the Emberton residence to inform them that further investigation at this time would only be re-contacting those interviewed previously and that no leads had been developed so far.
>
> "Should clues be developed by the clothing examination, the agency might again attempt to determine the circumstances surrounding Olene's death with these new leads. At this time, nothing can be done, we informed Mr. and Mrs. Emberton.
>
> "We returned to Indianapolis where this report was written and submitted."

Although it seems as if W.R.S. intended for the December 15 report to be his last, two additional notations were made. On December 23, W.R.S. contacted Sergeant Young of the Indiana State Police Crime Lab. According to the report, Young "stated the clothing analysis in the Olene Emberton case has not been completed. There has been several isolations of substances; however, no comparisons have been made to date."

That apparently seemed like a potential future lead worthy of pursuing, because on Friday, January 7, 1966, W.R.S. contacted

Sergeant Young again. The response was likely not what W.R.S. would have preferred. The agent wrote, "[Sgt. Young] stated he thought it would be better for contact to be made with Sheriff Verl Grimme because he is the only person that can release any information regarding the analysis of the Olene Emberton clothing."

According to the report, W.R.S. picked up the phone and called Grimme. After the call, W.R.S. recorded the following note: "Stated he had not received any report from the state police lab and had not sent anything for comparative analysis recently. The conversation was discontinued, and I wrote this report."

Because the January 7, 1966, report was the last known in existence, it appears Pinkerton's investigation ended there. The reason is open to conjecture.

During Ed Achenbach's interview in December 2016, he disclosed that one of his buddies, whose family operated a downtown Tipton donut shop in the mid-1960s, told him the Pinkerton detectives had been regular customers there. Achenbach said his friend told him the Pinkerton men often complained that Tipton was the most closely knit town they had ever worked.

Perhaps the Tipton community truly was impenetrable. Or perhaps, as the Embertons believed, Pinkerton's progress had been stymied from day one by a sheriff who refused to cooperate, hoarded leads, and withheld information in the event that, when the case finally broke, he alone could reap the glory.

Two months later, Roxie told the *Kokomo Tribune* that she and her husband were disappointed by the lack of assistance Pinkerton's received from the Tipton County sheriff. According to the February 16, 1966, *Tribune* story, the agency submitted its findings to Tipton County Prosecutor Richard Regnier with a complaint that Grimme would not work with them.

Perhaps Pinkerton's observation was correct and Grimme deliberately withheld information from the agency's investigator that might have proved fruitful. Or perhaps, as Grimme had repeatedly told the Embertons and the press, there was no solid evidence; there were no leads.

During a March 2006 telephone interview with Major Justus Littlejohn, then director of the Indiana State Police Crime Lab, he expressed interest in looking into the Emberton case with an eye toward possibly reopening it. However, he said, before he could launch a new investigation, he would need to locate the physical evidence. And that, he said, could be problematic.

"Things were a lot looser back in the '60s," Littlejohn said. "The way evidence was tracked in '65 is not how it is tracked now. Back then, they had what was called 'the black book.' Evidence was logged in and, later, some of it may have been logged out. And later, logged in again. It may have been spread over several pages. It was not a good way to track evidence."

Littlejohn vowed to do his best to find the black book. But as it turned out, he could not. Thus, the brick wall Grimme had run into forty years before had not budged. There was still no solid evidence; there were still no leads. •

> *"We will never give up. I had too good a girl for this to happen to her."*
> — Roxie Emberton

18
REWARD

Four months to the day that Olene disappeared, resolution of the case was still stalled. With her family's desperation for answers growing with each passing day, Floyd and Roxie took a new tack. They dug deep into their pockets and offered a reward. A page one story in the February 16, 1966, *Kokomo Tribune* reported that the "heartbroken" Emberton family was offering $5,000 "for information that leads to the apprehension and conviction of the person or persons responsible for the illegal disposing of Olene Emberton's body along the county road."

The irony of the reward was unconscionable. The Embertons had lost their daughter in a manner so foul, it was nearly impossible to imagine, but the only justice they could hope for was an indictment of illegal disposal. However, without evidence revealing the identity of whom Olene had met at the Green and North Streets intersection, or without a cause of death proving murder, the only prosecutable crime known to have been committed was the abandonment of her body along that road.

Floyd and Roxie Emberton announced the reward at a press conference at the Embertons' home to which only reporters from the Tipton and Kokomo papers were invited.

According to the *Tipton Tribune*, the Embertons were dissatisfied with the investigation conducted by law enforcement personnel, as well as the Pinkerton Detective Agency, which the Embertons had hired. They also felt the medical examiner had missed something during the autopsy. Floyd said he would be open to exhuming his daughter's body on the chance it would produce evidence that had been overlooked.

The *Tipton Tribune* stated Floyd and Roxie "expressed the fervent hope that this offer of a reward would cause someone to come forward with information which would lead to a solution."

The *Kokomo Tribune* story pointed out that the family's savings would be financing the entire $5,000 reward, and that Tipton attorney Joe Watson would be handling all the details.

In his November 2016 sit-down interview, Watson described the Emberton family as understandably "excitable." They had contacted him at the recommendation of a mutual acquaintance, Ted Morris, officer at Farmers Loan & Trust and husband of Floyd's cousin, Doris.

"They authorized me to set up a trust to pay something to somebody who knew what happened," Watson said, "since Grimme couldn't figure it out. [Floyd Emberton] was desperate to find out who did what."

Roxie and Floyd told the Tipton paper they were confident Olene had known the person she went with the night she disappeared. They expressed certainty that their daughter would never have gotten in a car with a stranger.

"She couldn't have disappeared as she did without someone having seen her and knowing who she was with," Roxie said. "We hope this reward will cause that person or persons who saw her to come forward with the information which will let us know what eventually happened."

Floyd and Roxie told the *Kokomo Tribune* about the anguish they had endured as they awaited justice for their daughter.

"Often I wake up in the middle of the night thinking about

this thing," Floyd said. "I can't get back to sleep."

Roxie spoke of her inability to sleep, too. "I think about it night and day. I dread for night to come."

Roxie told the *Tribune* that she hoped whoever caused Olene's death also had trouble sleeping.

"I don't see how they can get up and look in the mirror every day and not feel like screaming," she told the *Kokomo Tribune*. "Whoever got my daughter, killed a whole family."

Floyd swore that if the reward didn't produce the answer they ached to hear, they would try something else.

"This may take twenty years," Roxie said. "We will never give up. I had too good a girl for this to happen to her."

Added to the Emberton's $5,000 was the $500 reward that the *Kokomo Tribune* posted the previous November. Despite the generous amount, the reward, like the private detective they hired, produced nothing. However, two months later, a near-tragedy affecting another young, Tipton woman brought the Embertons, as well as Sheriff Verl Grimme, a brief modicum of optimism. •

This photo of Roxie and Floyd accompanied the February 6, 1966, Kokomo Tribune *story. (Reprinted with permission of the* Kokomo Tribune.*)*

> *"Questions were put to him regarding the death of Olene Emberton, but his replies, as in previous questioning, indicated he was not involved in that case."*
> —Tipton Tribune, April 28, 1966

19
A VIABLE SUSPECT EMERGES

An anxious young man telephoned the Tipton police station the evening of Monday, April 25, 1966, to report an assault on his wife by an intruder he knew quite well. Without delay, police officers confronted the woman's accused attacker at his North Main Street home and took him to jail.

The arrest of eighteen-year-old Perry Steven (Steve) Miller for assault and battery with intent to commit rape sparked immediate interest from local law enforcement officials. Was Miller the missing link to the Emberton case they had been looking for?

Miller was raised in Tipton County. As a youngster, he and his family lived near Hobbs, later moving to the southwest part of the county, not far up the road from the Embertons. In 1964, his parents bought a house on North Main Street and moved the family into town.

Miller had grown into an unspectacular-looking young man with curly, short-cropped blond hair, a deceptively winning smile, and a set of cobalt blue eyes that masked the malevolence roiling his soul. At six feet tall, he carried an imposing two hundred pounds of solid brawn with ease.

Miller attended school in Tipton through his junior year of high school and had excelled in sports, baseball primarily. Ironically, Miller's Little League baseball prowess was undoubtedly enhanced by the tutelage of an excellent coach — Tipton County's future sheriff, Verl Grimme.

Despite growing up in Tipton, Miller today is an enigma to most of his former classmates. Few remember him, although Olene's old friends, who lived in the same southwest area of rural Tipton County at the time Olene did, recalled Miller riding their school bus, the same bus Olene rode. Thus, there can be no doubt Miller and Olene were acquainted. In fact, evidence apparently written by Miller's own hand suggests they may have been friends.

The message Miller allegedly inscribed in Olene's 1964 Tipton High School yearbook, *The Tiptonian*, reads: To Olene | A real cute and sweet girl | stay that way always | (Promise) | Steve Miller | "65."

While there may be nothing significant behind it, the tender sentiment he allegedly wrote to her on the back of his class photo taken in early 1964 — To Olene, one of the nicest girls I know and

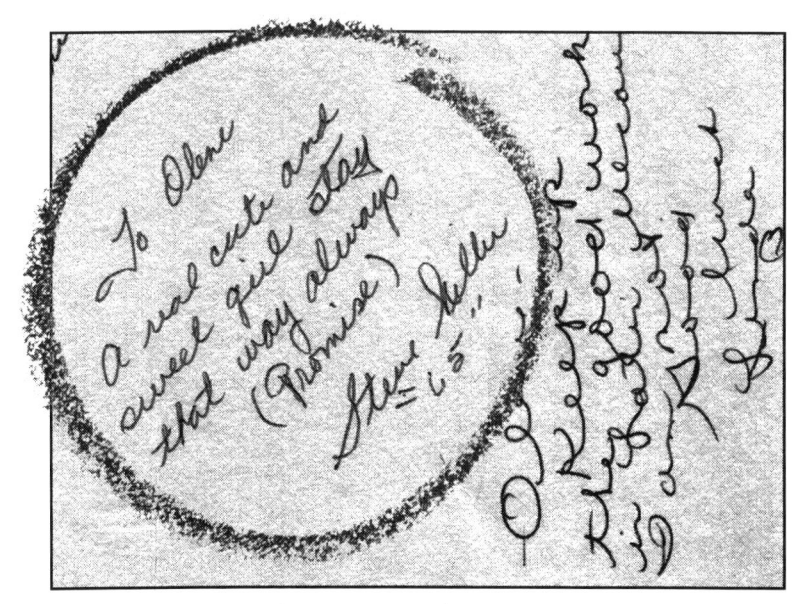

*Miller allegedly wrote this message to **Olene** in her 1964 high school yearbook. (Courtesy Debbie Emberton.)*

Steve Miller's 1964 class photo, taken when he was a Tipton High School junior, bears what appears to be his handwritten inscription to Olene on the back. It was found among Olene's personal effects after her death. (Courtesy Marty Talbert.)

like to be with and also who can understand me most of the time. Love always, Steve "65" — implies that Miller was at least smitten.

One of Olene's classmates believed she and Miller had dated in 1963 and possibly later. But based on two handwritten notes in her 1963 yearbook, under the inked-in header at the top of the Activities page, "Reserved for the one & only," it appears another boy had captured Olene's heart.

The Thursday, April 28, 1966, *Kokomo Tribune* carried the page one story about Miller's latest accusations under the headline, "Tipton Youth Admits Attempted Rape." The story began, "Perry Steven Miller, 18, 703 N. Main, Tipton, was arrested at 8 p.m. Monday [April 25] for assault and battery with intent to commit rape." It then laid out the details of the assault.

"Sometime after 4 p.m. Monday," the story read, "Miller entered a woman's apartment. When her husband returned home from work, he called police. The woman, about 18, was taken to the Tipton Hospital suffering mainly from shock. Miller, who is 6 foot, weighing 200 pounds, was a friend of her husband."

The victim's husband and Miller weren't simply casual acquaintances; they were close and had been for years. When the couple married in August of 1965, Miller served as a groomsman. The following December, it was Miller's turn to wed, and for best man, he selected his good buddy.

However, a mere four months later, Miller apparently had decided the friendship was dispensable and should not stand between him and the object of his alleged sexual desire.

Law enforcement officials from city, county and state took immediate note of the violent attack against the woman, who was barely over five feet tall and couldn't have weighed more than a hundred pounds. According to the *Kokomo Tribune* story, Miller spent Monday night in jail, and on Tuesday was treated to a round-trip, one hundred twenty-mile journey to Noble County in northern Indiana. The destination was the Indiana State Police post in Ligonier, where he was given a lie detector test. The *Kokomo Tribune* reported that, according to law enforcement officials, Miller admitted his guilt to the charges and signed a confession.

Nearly lost in the story was this reference to the Emberton case: "Miller was also questioned in connection with Olene Emberton … and was cleared of any implication in her death, Chief Pratt said."

The April 28 edition of the *Tipton Tribune* also reported the incident, but it included one additional, critically telling piece of information: "Questions were put to [Miller] regarding the death of Olene Emberton, but his replies, as in previous questioning, indicated he was not involved in that case."

That seemingly innocuous statement — "as in previous questioning" — revealed a crucial, never-before reported fact that at some early point in the investigation, law enforcement officials had considered Miller someone of interest, possibly someone responsible for Olene's death or, at the least, responsible for abandoning her body.

It was a stunning piece of information that begged the question: What had attracted the officials' attention in the first place? Whatever it had been, and when coupled with an absence of tangible evidence, it was obviously insufficient to justify further police investigation. The April 25 incident reinvigorated the original suspicion about Miller, and officers seized the opportunity by transporting him to Ligonier, the nearest state police post equipped to administer a polygraph test.

Among the local officials who accompanied Miller on the April 26 trek to Ligonier was then-Tipton Police Chief Jim Pratt. During his 2006 interview for this book, he spoke of the experience.

"I wasn't in the room when he did the test," Pratt said, referring to Miller. "I was standing outside. When they got through, a man came out and said, 'Well, he won't admit to anything, but my test shows that he knows about it [the Emberton case].' But he wouldn't discuss it other than the case we took him up there on [the April 25, 1966, assault]."

Pratt emphasized that the man who administered the polygraph test said Miller would answer only the questions related to his current arrest.

"He [Miller] wouldn't discuss anything else," Pratt said. "Grimme bought us dinner, and Miller made the remark, 'You're not going to get any more out of me feeding me than you would before.' We could talk about anything, other than what he was accused of, and he would sit there and just talk to you like a normal person. But when you tried to ask him something [about the Emberton case], he'd just sit there and not say a word."

Regardless of Miller's refusal to answer questions related to Olene, polygraph tests were inadmissible in court. Thus, without a confession or evidence linking Miller to Olene's death, Grimme apparently could not justify pursuing him further in the Emberton case.

Miller was arraigned May 13 for assault and battery with intent to commit rape, and through his attorney, Horace Holmes, he pleaded "not guilty." A tentative date for a jury trial was set for July 25 but was later moved to December.

* * *

On November 28, Miller withdrew his "not guilty" plea. Withdrawing his plea was essentially admitting guilt, which was a curious move leading legal minds to wonder if Miller's attorney had struck a deal with the prosecutor that would have been played out at the trial, set for December 19. However, the case wasn't tried on that date; rather, it was continued indefinitely to await the return of the victim's husband, who had been deployed to Vietnam with his Army unit.

In a curious move, Miller's attorney filed a "Motion to Suppress Evidence" with the county clerk on January 10, 1967. Highlights of the motion follow.

> "… his constitutional rights were infringed upon in that he was held in the said Tipton County jail incommunicado, refused the right of counsel, refused the right of consultation with his parents and his wife, that he was not taken before any judge or magistrate, that he was not advised of his right to secure and be represented by counsel, that he was not advised of his right to remain silent, nor was he advised that any statement he might make could be used as evidence against him."

The court document stated that Miller further complained that shortly after his arrival at the Tipton County jail at 9:00 p.m. April 25, 1966, he was surrounded by officers of the Tipton Police, Tipton

County Sheriff's Department, and Indiana State Police, as well as the Tipton County Prosecutor. "... all of whom," the document states, "intensively interrogated and questioned this Defendant from the time of his arrest until 2:30 a.m. on April 26, 1966, at which time the Defendant was placed in a cell in the said Tipton County jail."

The document goes on to describe the interrogation at the State Police post in Ligonier.

> "The Defendant says that at or about 9:00 o'clock a.m. on the 26th day of April 1966, he was removed from the said Tipton County jail by the peace and police officers of the City of Tipton and of Tipton County, Indiana, and placed in a Sheriff's car with such peace and police officers and the Tipton County Prosecuting Attorney and taken without his consent to Ligonier, Indiana, a distance of approximately 120 to 130 miles from the Tipton County jail, and to the Ligonier Post of the Indiana State Police at which place, the said defendant was again intensively interrogated and questioned by officers of the Tipton County Sheriff's Department, and the Tipton County Prosecuting Attorney continuously and without respite until after midnight of the said 26th day of April, 1966, during all of which said time no explanation was made to the Defendant by any of the peace or police officers or Prosecuting Official, that he, the Defendant, could remain silent, that he, the said Defendant, could refuse to answer questions, that if the said Defendant did answer questions or make any statement that the same could be used as evidence against him, or that he, the Defendant, was entitled to have the services of consultation with, and advice from, an attorney."

No response to this motion could be located at the Tipton

County Clerk's office. If the point was suppression of evidence connected to the assault-and-battery-with-intent-to-commit-rape case, the motion was likely denied since the case was subsequently continued.

* * *

For the next three years, awaiting his trial, Miller managed to keep his name out of the press. It reappeared May 22, 1969, when local papers reported that he had been arrested for the abduction and rape of a nineteen-year-old Hamilton County woman. Four days later, several papers reported yet another incident, this one involving the abduction of a teenaged Elwood girl the previous month.

The first of the two incidents occurred at an Elwood Laundromat the night of April 27, 1969. According to a May 28, 1969, report in the *Elwood Call Leader* and the victim's testimony at Miller's subsequent trial, he had armed himself with a lifelike toy gun and attacked a fifteen-year-old girl from behind and forced her into his car. He then drove her to a remote part of the Tipton County countryside and, pressing the gun to her neck, forced her to perform oral sex.

The next attack took place May 16 in rural Arcadia. The September 12, 1969, *Tipton Tribune* reported that Miller pretended his car had broken down alongside a Hamilton County side road. When the nineteen-year-old Good Samaritan stopped to help, he wielded a handgun, climbed into her car, and ordered her to drive to a secluded, wooded area. There he ripped off her clothing with a box cutter, tied her to a tree, forced her to perform oral sex, and raped her. When he was finished, he threatened to kill her if she told anyone what had happened. She convinced him that she wouldn't tell, and he let her go.

Miller was arrested five days later, along with the victim's father and grandfather, who had shown up uninvited at Miller's front door brandishing a firearm and loaded for bear. The two were preparing to tie up Miller when police arrived.

Miller was transferred to the Hamilton County jail in Noblesville, and bond was set at $30,500. The victim's father and grandfather were released.

Verl Grimme had been in the process of preparing a case against Miller for the alleged Elwood incident when the kidnapping and rape took place in Hamilton County. On May 26, Grimme filed a warrant with the Tipton County Circuit Court for a search at Miller's home. He served the warrant the same day. His handwritten note on the reverse side of the warrant (below) lists the four items — all of them children's toys — included in his search. They were: one Pal – Daisy (play pistol) chrome, one Pal – KilGore (play pistol) chrome, one 45 automatic (Nichol – cap or play), and one Raggedy Ann Doll – Polkadot blue and white dress.

> Served this Search Warrant this 26th day of May 1969 by going to 343 Conde St Tipton Ind about 0 and finding the following articles:
> 1 - Pal - Daisy (play pistol) chrome
> 1 - Pal - KilGore (play pistol) chrome
> 1 - 45 Automatic (Nichol - cap or play
> 1 - Raggedy ann Doll - polka Dot Blue & white dots
> and now return this Writ this 27th day of May 1969
> Verl Grimme
> Sheriff Tipton Co.

While Miller was preparing his legal strategy for the April 26 and May 16, 1969, crimes for which he was charged, his April 1966 assault case was still pending.

The Arcadia case went to trial in Hamilton County on Friday, September 12, 1969. It was initially expected to last one day, but there were more witnesses than expected, and the case didn't go to the jury until the seventh day. Miller took the stand on Monday,

September 15 and testified with a straight face that he had not forced the Arcadia woman to drive him to the wooded area, where he attacked her. Claiming she had told him that she would go with him "for a price," he also alleged, "There was no force. She was willing."

After just four hours of deliberation on Wednesday, September 17, the jury of three women and nine men found Miller guilty on four counts: kidnap, which carries a sentence of mandatory life imprisonment, sodomy, rape, and auto banditry. The *Tipton Tribune* reported, "Miller appeared somewhat stunned as the guilty verdict was read."

At 10:00 a.m., Wednesday, October 8, 1969, Miller returned to Judge Sue Shields' courtroom for formal sentencing: life in prison, as mandated by Indiana statute. Immediately after, he was transported to the Indiana State Prison at Michigan City. Due to his sentence, the other two cases were later discharged, and a parole hearing in 1971 reaped him no reward.

* * *

Miller's sexual crimes against women are what paved his path to prison, but his calculated charm is what duped the Indiana Parole Board into setting him free less than twenty years later.

Two and a half years after his 1988 release, in a stunning affront to the state's decision to give him a second chance, Miller, then forty-three and accompanied by two males less than half his age, one of them his stepson, abducted a nineteen-year-old woman from a Valparaiso convenience store at 1:30 a.m. November 14, 1990. From there, they transported her to a construction site in northern Porter County, where Miller ordered the boys to torture, beat, rape, and shoot her execution style with a shotgun. The teenaged boys were apprehended two days later in Owensboro, Kentucky. Miller was arrested three days later, November 17, at his home in La Porte, where police found him in his backyard cowering in a hole he had covered with leaves.

Miller's trial began Tuesday, April 2, 1991, in Porter Superior Court in Valparaiso. The *Tipton Tribune* carried a local story about Miller on April 13, 1991. *Tribune* reporter Ron Wilkins interviewed Miller's victim of the 1969 kidnapping and rape in Hamilton County that resulted in the life sentence from which Miller was paroled in 1988. The woman said that for six years during the 1980s, she had pleaded with the Indiana Parole Board not to release him. If only Miller had remained in prison, she said, the Valparaiso woman's murder could have been prevented.

The *Tribune* writer continued his story, bringing out some astonishing revelations that should have been of particular interest to Tipton residents who remembered the mysterious death of Olene Emberton. Wilkins wrote:

> "The victim said that during the abduction, Miller made statements implying the 1969 abduction and rape was not his first time. She added he made statements that led her to believe he may have been involved in an October 1965 death of a Tipton teenager.
>
> "Jim Bradley, an Indiana State Police Trooper at the time, investigated the 1969 Hamilton County rape and also the October 1965 death. Bradley said Miller was a suspect in the 1965 death, but investigators were never able to build a strong case to support that conclusion.
>
> "Richard Regnier, who was Tipton County Prosecutor during the 1965 investigation, also confirmed Miller was a suspect, but he said Miller denied involvement when he was questioned by authorities."

On Wednesday, April 17, 1991, the jury of six men and six women found Miller guilty of his horrific, November 14, 1990, assault against the young woman, and it netted him the death penalty. He was returned to the Indiana State Prison in Michigan

City to await execution.

* * *

After Miller was convicted, Porter County's probation department launched its pre-sentence investigation, a probe into the convicted person's history to determine if there were special circumstances that should tamp down the harshness of the forthcoming punishment. Former Howard County Sheriff Marty Talbert, then an investigator with the Indiana State Police, was looking into Miller's past arrests and convictions in Tipton and Hamilton counties. Talbert had two primary contacts there. One was I.S.P. Officer Jim Bradley; the other was Roxie Emberton.

When Talbert visited with Roxie at her home, she gave him Miller's eleventh grade school photo bearing the handwritten message to her daughter on the back. Talbert believed she had preserved the photo in hopes of eventually meeting someone with the law enforcement authority and prowess to grasp what the picture suggested. Talbert recognized the photo as a key that might possibly unlock the decades old, unsolved Emberton case.

"There was always suspicion that [Miller] had knowledge of the [Olene] case," Talbert said. "He was obviously going to get life in prison or the death penalty on account of the Porter County murder. There was nothing for him to lose by discussing the case, so I thought I'd take a shot at talking to him."

Talbert met with Miller the morning of Wednesday, June 30, 1993, at the Indiana State Prison in Michigan City. Talbert recounted the meeting.

> "They brought Miller down. He was in prison garb with leg shackles, a belly belt, and handcuffs. They read him his rights, and he was more businesslike than anything — not warm and friendly, sort of matter-of-fact, saying, 'I've already talked about this. ... I don't

know why you're here. ... I didn't know [Olene] well.'

"I told him the picture seemed to indicate he did know her well. It's hard to recall everything said in our conversation, but he didn't want to talk about it and was adamant that he'd been down this road before.

"I tried different approaches: 'The family would like some closure'; 'Roxie would like to know what happened to her daughter'; I'm not here to arrest you; I just want to know about Olene.'

"The interview didn't last all that long. If you look at his history, he's not a confessor, but it was worth making an attempt to get it resolved. My main interest was to get the family some closure. It wasn't a waste of time, considering the circumstances.

"There are a number of people who have been convicted and sentenced to life who make an admission about other activities. But it won't happen until there's no chance for them to see freedom again."

That was the only time Talbert spoke with Miller, but his interest in the Emberton case has never waned.

* * *

After years of appeals, in 2001 Miller's death sentence was commuted to life without possibility of parole. Today, he is incarcerated at the Miami Correctional Facility in Bunker Hill, Indiana.

Miller was contacted twice in 2016 with requests for a personal interview for this book about his memories of Olene and her mysterious death. He declined both requests. However, when Tipton County Deputy Mike Tarrh made a similar request in May of 2018, Miller accepted.

Tarrh, a thirty-four-year veteran of the Indiana State Police, spent sixteen years as a detective investigating a variety of cases, including cold case murders. He joined the Tipton County

Sheriff's Department in 2015.

He became aware of the Emberton case in the spring of 2017 and spent the next several months trying to tie up loose ends in hopes of giving closure to Olene's family and friends. He spoke with witnesses and looked for the missing case files, the physical evidence, and the autopsy report. By the spring of 2018, however, Tarrh conceded that his pursuit of Olene's justice had led him to the same brick wall that Tipton County Sheriff Verl Grimme had hit more than fifty years before. Yet Tarrh wasn't ready to concede. He saw one more chance to secure the elusive answers. He requested an interview with Steve Miller. The two met May 16 at the prison in Miami County.

"I told him I was trying to do something positive, trying to get answers for Olene's family and a group of her friends," Tarrh reported afterward. Throughout the interview, which lasted just over an hour, "Miller was extremely polite and under control," Tarrh said.

Tarrh refreshed Miller's memory about the case and asked questions he hoped would result in new information or an admission of wrong-doing.

Nevertheless, according to Tarrh, Miller denied any involvement in Emberton's death or possessing any knowledge about it.

"Nothing seemed to faze him," Tarrh said. "He wouldn't take responsibility for the two convictions that got him two life sentences either."

Learning nothing new and breaking no new ground, Tarrh was disappointed but still hopeful.

"I left on good terms," he said. "I told him to let me know if he thinks of anything that could help. The outcome of our meeting wasn't my goal, but you don't accomplish anything if you don't try." •

20
AUTHOR'S POINT OF VIEW: NINE MINUTES

Mention the word "psychic," and the likes of Theresa Caputo of reality TV's "Long Island Medium" fame, Allison DuBoise, the inspiration behind NBC's long-running series "Medium," and James Van Praagh, bestselling psychic author and television personality, come to mind.

While the intuitive abilities of highly celebrated psychics may provide endless fascination for connoisseurs of parapsychology, not everyone is convinced. Historically, clairvoyants are better known for getting rich off their clients' naïveté than they are for picking winning Lottery numbers. Yet as far-fetched as it may seem to the doubters among us, consulting with psychics is not always the last-ditch exercise of the hopelessly naïve or desperate.

Take the Central Intelligence Agency for example. In late 1995, the nation's top intelligence organization released a highly classified report titled, "An Evaluation of Remote Viewing: Research and Applications." It revealed that the C.I.A. had employed psychics for more than twenty years to engage in "remote viewing," a questionable exercise used to collect military intelligence on hostile countries. According to a November 12, 2015, *Newsweek* article, the $20 million program had hired psychics "to visualize hidden extremist training sites in Libya, describe new Soviet submarine designs, and to pinpoint the locations of U.S. hostages held by foreign kidnappers." The report stated that although the operation, code-named Star Gate, had produced "something beyond odd statistical hiccups," the intel it produced was too "vague and ambiguous" to merit actionable follow up.

Regardless of the report's dubious conclusion, the C.I.A. didn't stop its research into whether telepathy could be a dependable investigative tool. A 1998 document titled, "Use of Psychics in Law Enforcement," divulges a study made with officers at eleven police agencies that had claimed success in working with psychics. The report cites an above-average success record, stating that, "Eight of the officers said the psychic provided them with otherwise unknown information which was helpful to the case." But the report urged investigators to use sound judgment when seeking the services of a psychic.

"Even talented psychics cannot be accurate 100 percent of the time," it stated. "The key to good results is careful selection."

The C.I.A.'s report pointed out that "a bad choice might be more of a hindrance than a help." It followed with a list of criteria for picking a psychic whose track record aligns with the case, while urging investigators to steer clear of psychics that are more interested in notoriety or money than in solving the case.

"Many psychics, who are primarily interested in using their ability to help others, wish to remain anonymous," the report emphasized.

The feasibility of using psychics as an investigative adjunct wasn't a new concept when the C.I.A. released its report in 1998. The research had been going on for years. The May 1979 edition of *The Police Chief* magazine ran an article titled, "Managing the Psychic in Criminal Investigations," encouraging police executives to embrace psychic phenomena as a potential investigative tool worthy of further experimentation and research. "Perhaps in this way," the article stated, "the investigative role of the psychic will ultimately be more clearly defined."

The idea had occurred to even *me* four years before that, while I was conference coordinator for the International Security Conference, sponsored by Security World Publishing, based in Los Angeles, California. A close friend of mine at the time was acquainted with famed, Kentucky-based radio psychic David Hoy. I thought it would be interesting to offer a workshop teaching security professionals how to hone their innate psychic abilities as a supplement to the traditional security techniques at their disposal, such as alarms, closed-circuit television, and uniformed guards. I presented the idea to my boss, and to my great surprise, he said yes. We offered Hoy's workshop at our next conference, meeting at the New York Hilton, located in downtown New York City. The day of the workshop arrived, and although the classroom could have comfortably accommodated a hundred people, five attended. Not five hundred … *five*. It was a humiliating bust. Nonetheless, my gracious boss thanked me for my innovative ingenuity but never again rowed the I.S.C.'s boat into the uncharted waters of psychic security.

Virtually no one in the mid-1960s' Tipton suspected that any member of their law enforcement agencies would so much as consider the use of unconventional crime-solving tools. According to Joe Watson, his friend Sheriff Verl Grimme did more than consider it, although Grimme's motivation likely was fueled by desperation rather than innovation.

During my November 2016 interview with Watson, he told me, "Verl contacted a lady from around Frankfort — a clairvoyant. He wanted to see what she could come up with. He was straining to get the truth."

Roxie Emberton also followed the unconventional route, contacting an unknown number of psychics, according to her daughter-in-law, Debbie. Although, as Debbie reported, "None ever told Roxie anything that helped."

* * *

I first thought of consulting a psychic about Olene's death in the early spring of 2017 after a friend told me about a relative who, she said, possessed highly attuned sensory instincts. According to my friend, when her family had been desperately looking for her missing brother, they sought the relative's input. Despite the unfortunate outcome of the family's search, the leads their relative provided had proved amazingly accurate. My friend spoke of other incidents, as well, that put her relative's intuitive skills to the test, and each provided further confirmation of an exceptional extrasensory ability.

My first conversation with the psychic woman took place in mid-April 2017. We talked by phone, and I told her a bit about myself and my interest in Olene's case. I limited the specifics about the case to Olene's name, age, and date of death. She expressed an interest in helping and told me she was already picking up messages. She lived south of Indianapolis and wouldn't be available to come to Tipton for about two weeks. We agreed to meet at my house Sunday afternoon, April 30. She asked that I withhold her name out of concerns for her and her family's privacy, and I agreed. Thus, in keeping with her request, I am referring to her by the fictitious name of Connie throughout the account of our meeting and our conversations.

Following are my notes taken that day.

> Connie arrived with her daughter and two nieces around 2:30 p.m. She is a tiny, blonde-hair woman in her late sixties, and very pleasant. I walked outside to meet her, and she immediately asked for water. She said she was feeling a little queasy. She said the feeling started as soon as they pulled into my driveway. She said she was experiencing great sadness. I told her I wasn't sad, and she explained that the sadness was coming from

the Olene tragedy.

Connie and her daughter climbed into my car — Connie in the front seat, her daughter in the back. I told them I would drive Olene's last known route — from Main Street, west on North Street to Green, where she had abandoned her car. During our phone conversation, Connie said she had "seen" someone watching Olene. Today, she said the person might have been Olene's date standing on the sidewalk watching her drive away.

When we drove past the four-way stop at North and Green Streets, Connie said she didn't think Olene had parked her car there; that someone else had parked it. Later, she said the person Olene met there may have been on foot, or maybe driving a pickup truck. (However, it should be noted that Jennifer Cels, who had lived in the house next to where Olene's car was parked, said that her mother arrived home sometime after midnight the night Olene went missing and commented on the unfamiliar, red Chevy parked in front of their house.)

From there, I continued west to Sweetland Avenue, where I turned left and drove slowly by the former Emberton home. Connie said she was getting nothing, so I headed east again on North Street. Our next stop would be the county road where Olene's body had been found. During the drive, Connie said she felt there had been another young woman, who Olene's assailant had assaulted around that same time as Olene's death. Connie said she felt the suspect was in his twenties and described him as having "crystal eyes." She felt he had been athletic.

When I turned onto the narrow lane in the northeastern section of Tipton County, Connie pointed to the south toward a nearby woods. When we talked by phone, she mentioned that a wooded area held a significance, but she was uncertain as to what. As I slowly proceeded up the road, I told her I didn't know exactly where Olene had been found. We had traveled about a third of the mile-long road, when Connie told me to stop because we had just passed the spot where Olene had lain. I backed up, and we sat in the car quietly for a minute or so.

She said Olene had not died on this road, that she died somewhere else and had been moved there. Since our first conversation, I had told Connie very little about Olene and virtually nothing about the circumstances of her death. I don't recall telling Connie any other details until she either spoke of them on her own that day or asked questions.

At this point, I turned on my tape recorder, and the following is a direct transcription of what Connie said.

> "This is crude, and I don't mean to offend anybody, but I have thought this for quite a while… I'm picturing it actually. He [the assailant] was forcing her to [perform a sex act]. He was very forceful, and she suffocated. I don't know if that makes sense. … Her hyoid bone was cracked. I don't know that it was completely broken. He was sitting on her. It was to the point she couldn't bite or fight him off or anything like that. I think he was so surprised that she died and that *that* had happened … it was almost accidental, and he didn't know what to do. … [Pause of about twenty seconds] …

Okay, we're going to have to go. [At this point, Connie is experiencing trouble breathing.] That's what it is about ... the breathing, and that's what she was experiencing."

I started driving, and when I looked over at Connie, I noticed she was shedding tears. Back at my house, Connie, her daughter, and I met with her two nieces, our mutual friend, and Debbie Emberton. We recounted the impressions Connie had picked up during our drive, and then we all unwound with some laughter and talked about topics unrelated to the case.

As Connie was leaving my house about an hour later, I extended my deep appreciation for her help and invited her to keep in touch.

I next spoke with Connie when she phoned me a month and a half later, in mid-June, to let me know about the new messages she had recently received from Olene.

Olene had been on her mind lately, she said, but while passing through the area two days before, the sense of Olene's presence had been quite strong.

"It was like we were connected," she said.

During our conversation, Connie reiterated her belief that Olene's death had been accidental. She stressed again that murder was not her assailant's intent when he met Olene at that four-way stop and persuaded her to go for a ride. Connie was certain Olene had been the victim of a sexual assault, and that she had suffocated while her attacker lost control.

Connie said she believed the "main investigator," Sheriff Verl Grimme, picked up on "a lot of things" about the case, but other people brushed them aside.

"They were in so much awe and bewilderment," she said.

"They were overwhelmed and wanted to go with the obvious."

Connie added that Olene's assailant "laughs because he got away with it."

At the time of our June conversation, I had taken a temporary leave from the Olene project to prepare for the approaching release of my novel. Imagine my reaction when Connie told me Olene was growing impatient with me.

"Olene is concerned because you stopped writing," Connie said, adding, "but once you start writing again, you'll think of things and put the research together."

One other piece of information Connie related during that June conversation gave me chills.

"Olene wants you to call the book 'Nine Minutes,'" she said.

"Why?" I asked.

"That's how long it took her to die." •

> *"In loving memory of Olene Emberton ..."*
> — The Emberton Family

21
ANNIVERSARY REMEMBRANCES

On October 18, 1966, both Kokomo papers published lengthy, page one, anniversary pieces reviewing the Emberton case, one of them co-written by the *Kokomo Morning Times*' seasoned editor, Bill Nangle, and a young, newly hired reporter named Don Havens. (Forty-six years later, Havens would embark on his first of two terms serving Tipton, his hometown, as its mayor.)

"Confused silence surrounds the first anniversary of the death of Olene Emberton," Nangle and Havens wrote, "with Sheriff Grimme the only police official still actively investigating the mysterious death of the then 17-year-old girl."

Their story commented on the inordinate number of rumors that Grimme had checked out. But ultimately, they concluded that the rumors served only to hinder the investigation.

"More than 250 pages in reports are on file at [Grimme's] office," the reporters wrote.

Over the past year, they continued, Grimme shared the case with outside law enforcement professionals, including the F.B.I., and asked for feedback.

"They relate that a thorough investigation was conducted," Nangle and Havens stated.

Their story continued with a quote from Grimme: "I have

welcomed the study and opinions of all the qualified investigators. They have helped by assuring us that the matter has been handled properly."

Grimme went on to say that he "won't rest until the case is brought before the court."

The *Kokomo Tribune* also ran a page one, anniversary story, which poignantly ended with this quote from Grimme: "We are still checking out tips and rumors every day. I'll go on with this case as long as there's a breath left in me. It's like a chain with a missing link, and someday we'll find that link."

The Emberton family observed the first anniversary of Olene's death with an "In Memoriam" in the *Tipton Tribune*. It read:

> In loving memory of Olene Emberton,
> Who left us Oct. 17, 1965.
> Just when her life was brightest,
> Just when her years were best,
> She was called from this world of sorrow,
> To her home in Heaven, to rest.
> She loved life so very much.
> Loved all it had to give.
> But for some unknown reason,
> She lost the right to live.
> No one knows the silent heartache.
> Only those who have lost can tell
> Of the grief we bear in silence,
> For our daughter we loved so well.
>
> Sadly missed by Father, Mother, Brothers Wayne,
> David and Bobby

Observing the second anniversary of Olene's death, the *Kokomo Morning Times* ran a page one piece on Tuesday, October 17, 1967.

Written by one of the paper's stringers, Tipton Junior High School science teacher Dave McGaw, it was headlined, "Father Plans Private Investigation on Anniversary of Emberton's Death." The story started, "The death of a Tipton County girl on Oct. 18 [sic], 1965, may still be solved, if the determination of her father proves victor over a cloud of unsolved odds."

McGaw reported that Floyd Emberton had told him during a phone interview of his plan to "seek additional investigation by a professional agency in the near future." Floyd expressed optimism that the case would be solved but maintained his criticism of Grimme's efforts.

"Sheriff Grimme has never done everything he could to solve this," Emberton said, according to McGaw.

In the interest of balance, the story countered Floyd's claim with a reminder that the Indiana State Police "praised" Grimme's investigation and his dedication to finding the solution. McGaw also asserted a previously unreported claim that Grimme had been offered employment at a private investigative firm "for his outstanding work on the case."

Grimme never went to work for a private investigation firm.

The *Kokomo Morning Times'* story ended with a dash of hope, opining that the nagging, unanswered questions concerning what happened to Olene will be answered "someday."

After that, Olene's name appeared in newsprint only on the anniversaries of her death in the "In Memoriam" column deep inside the *Tipton Tribune*.

It's a sad commentary on a tragedy that snuffed out a beautiful life and left many others in ruins. Attention spans are short, lives continue, and people move on. •

> "*I think it's a crying shame that she never got any justice ...*"
> — Gail Wix

22
FINAL THOUGHTS

When the Emberton case broke in October of 1965, Verl Grimme was nearing the end of his first four-year term as Tipton County sheriff. He started his second term in January of '67, but another four years were insufficient for him to close the case. As he complained many times, he never received a lead that didn't steer him down a path to nowhere. Former Tipton Police Officer Randy Horton, who considered Grimme his mentor, recalled that once Grimme left office, he never mentioned the case again.

"Once it was over and done," Horton said, "Verl didn't talk about it anymore."

Most deeply affected by Olene's death were her parents, of course. They mourned her until the day they died.

Many of Olene's friends and classmates say the trauma of her death has stuck with them throughout their lives, nagging at them, reminding them that danger can lurk anywhere, stirring up worry for their loved ones' safety. Conversely, others who left Tipton left the tragedy behind.

"I did follow the news of her death," Jill Edgar wrote. "I felt the horror and speculation over all of the rumors being spread. I remember discussing her death with my parents, which now, having been a parent, I can remember seeing the fear on their faces and the tremor in their voices that the same thing might happen to their little girl."

Edgar continued, "Back then, the lifestyle was so different than we live now. The news is so full of horrible things that we are deadened to the horror. But during our high school years, something of this scope was *exciting* for lack of a more sensitive word."

Sharon Foland said her parents shortened their rein on her after Olene's death.

"I always had to be home by a certain time," Foland said, "but after Olene died, being home when [my parents] said became a bigger deal. When this happened, they were like 'it could have been *you.*'"

Patricia Brooks took what happened to her friend to heart. Olene's mysterious death served Brooks as a compass for her common sense, sharpening her observation skills and guiding her judgment when circumstances seemed a bit off.

"In the years after Olene's death," Brooks wrote, "I was more aware of my surroundings."

Many members of Olene's class viewed the tragedy as the marker for a coming, dangerous era of innocence lost, while others, such as Jim Harmon, downplayed the odds of being victimized by rare, unanticipated evils.

"I must admit answering these questions [about Olene's unsolved death] brought back a lot of unpleasant thoughts and memories," Harmon wrote in his February 2017 email. "It was a very sad time for everyone, [but] after Olene's death, I never felt unsafe in Tipton. I kind of considered this event as a once-in-a-lifetime tragedy in our small, little town."

Continuing, he wrote, "What a tragedy that Olene's life was taken from her at such a young age. At the same time, it reminded me of how close our class was, and even if you didn't have a close relationship with certain classmates, we were still all a family of kids that grew up in Tipton and shared our formative years together — the good, the bad, and the ugly!"

Jennifer Cels, like Harmon, couldn't recall feeling vulnerable after the loss of her classmate.

"I never was frightened," she said. "I never thought there was a murderer out there. Maybe that was naiveté. I don't know why I didn't."

Terry Conwell doesn't recall feeling afraid either. "Of course," she added, "Mom kept good tabs on us."

Floetta Scelta had a different take.

"As far as affecting my life, I believe it did," Scelta wrote. "It's probably why I studied psychology and criminal justice in college. I always felt they should have solved this case. In today's world, it would have been solved."

In a 2016 letter, Gail Wix expressed distress that Olene's case remains open. She wrote:

> "I think it's a crying shame that [Olene] never got any justice for what was done to her. It's been 51 years now, and no one knows anything? This mystery has gone on too long, and I hope all of us care enough to keep these questions coming! Even if the guilty person is long dead, for the sake of Olene, and all of us who still think of her, we would like to know the name of the murderer. Maybe then, we can rest a little bit easier."

During a February 2017 telephone interview, Doris Morris — Floyd Emberton's first cousin — revealed her deep regret that she never knew what prevented Olene from arriving home that Saturday night.

"That's just it," Morris said. "I don't know what happened."

Morris recalled that Floyd and Roxie Emberton's anguish over losing their daughter was intensified by never knowing who had stopped her, why she had gone with them, and what caused her to die.

"Somewhere along the line," Morris said, "I heard my mother (Olean Jackson) and others ask, 'Who would Olene have gotten into a car with?' Personally, I don't think the person she was with meant to hurt her. I think they cared about her, or they wouldn't have folded her clothes. In my heart, I think it might have been accidental."

Morris said her mother, who was Olene's great-aunt and extremely close to the Emberton family, had experienced several dreams that were as sad as they were haunting.

"My mother often dreamed about Olene," Morris said. "She was so fond of her and could never get her off her mind. One time, my mom was so distraught over some dreams she'd had. In them, Olene talked to her and kept pointing, but Mom couldn't understand what she was saying."

Because her mother was adamant that Olene was reaching out to her, Morris told the Tipton County Prosecutor Richard Regnier about the dreams. He merely shrugged them off.

"But Mom believed it," she said. "It was like Olene was trying to tell her something. — 'Can't you see? Can't you see?' She wanted us to know something, but Mom couldn't make sense out of what she was trying to say."

The dreams continued sporadically for several months until, apparently, Olene simply gave up.

"Mom said that in her last dream, Olene didn't speak," Morris said. "It was all gestures and pointing at things, but Mom still couldn't understand. Finally, Olene just shrugged her little shoulders and turned and walked away. And that was the last dream." •

23
EPILOGUE: MURDER OR MISDEMEANOR?

In the fifty-plus years since Olene Emberton's death, her loved ones who grieve for her have never stopped asking what happened: Why did she take that right turn onto Green Street? Who was there waiting for her? Why did she leave her car? Where did she go? Why did she die? Who discarded her body in the tall grass next to that cornfield? Was that person guilty of murder or merely a misdemeanor?

What became of that one person, that sole keeper of all the answers? Did he die, leaving Olene's death a mystery for the ages? Or is he still living? And if he is, can he be persuaded to finally tell what happened and, at long last, give closure to her loved ones? Or will he selfishly take those final moments of Olene's life to his grave?

People tend to believe they can distinguish the evil monsters from the good guys, but the scary truth is, too often they can't. You don't have to live in a big city to encounter a psychotic killer. Sometimes they are impossible to detect. Sometimes they live in your hometown and display all the characteristics of the boy or girl next door.

The answers to all the questions surrounding Olene's death

could be just as near. Perhaps they've been lying dormant all these years, waiting to be awakened by an unknown witness' sudden recollection or the guilty person's sudden wave of conscience.

If such an awakening is conceivable, it had best happen soon, before the opportunity is lost forever.

Until then, the clock goes on ticking, and the overriding mystery continues to elude.

Murder or misdemeanor?

We may never know. •

R.I.P., Olene

DIAGRAMS OF TIPTON & TIPTON COUNTY NOTING LOCATIONS RELEVANT TO THE EMBERTON CASE

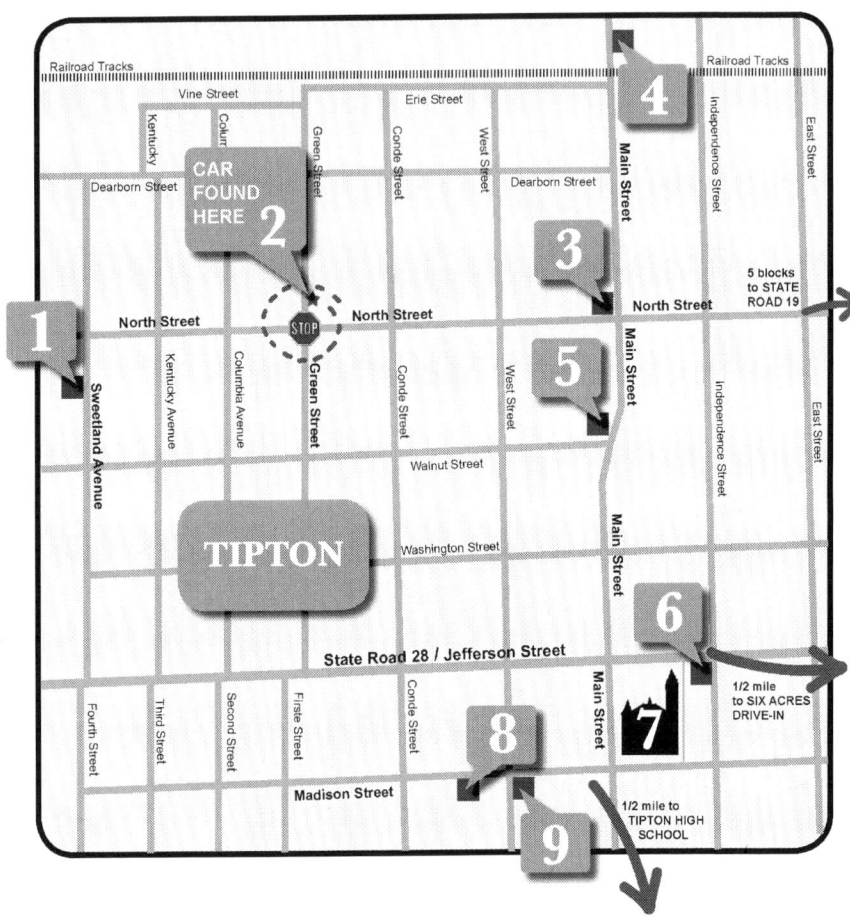

1. **Emberton House**, 336 Sweetland Avenue
2. **Olene's Car Found**, 2 doors north of 4-way stop at Green & North Streets
3. **Roudebush House**, 404 N. Main Street
4. **Miller House**, 703 N. Main Street
5. **Funeral Home**, 314 N. Main Street
6. **Diana Theatre**, 137 E. Jefferson Street
7. **Tipton County Courthouse**
8. **Preston House**, 221 W. Madison Street
9. **Tipton County Jail**, 121 W. Madison Street

161

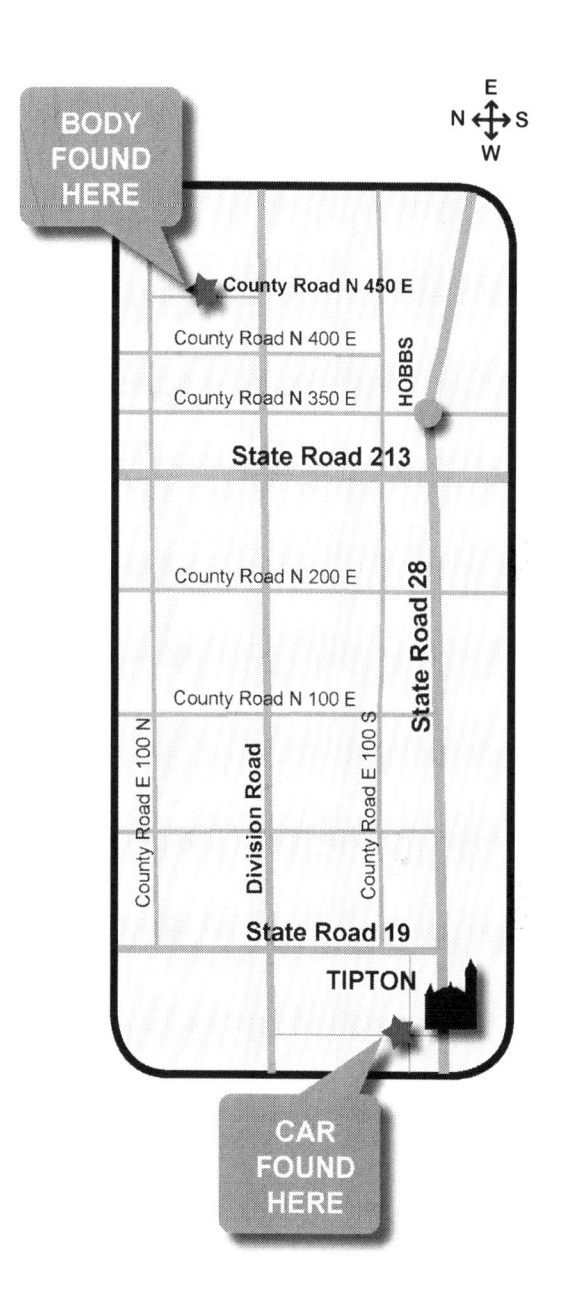

Timeline

SATURDAY
OCTOBER 16, 1965

2:00 p.m.	Olene attends wedding of frends Mollie Reecer and Mike Russell.	Church of Christ, East Jefferson Street
4:00 p.m.	Olene attends wedding reception.	Tom's Cafeteria, West Jefferson Street
7:00 p.m.	Olene and Phil Roudebush arrive at movie.	Diana Theatre 137 E. Jefferson St.
10:15 p.m.	Movie ends, and Olene and Phil drive around local drive-in.	Six Acre Drive-in on Tipton's far east side
10:20 p.m.	Olene sees brother Floyd Wayne walking along Jefferson Street and gives him a ride home.	Downtown Tipton
10:30 p.m.	Roxie Emberton hears someone enter the house. She assumes it's Olene, but it's Floyd Wayne.	Emberton Home, 336 Sweetland Ave.
	Olene drives Phil home, and they sit in her car and talk awhile.	Roudebush home, 404 N. Main St. at intersection with North Street
11:30 p.m.	Olene and Phil say goodnight. Phil climbs out of Olene's car and watches as she drives away, west on North Street, headed for home.	Roudebush home, 404 N. Main St. at intersection with North Street
12:30 a.m.	Mary Wiggins arrives home and notices the red car parked in front of her house in the 400 block of Green Street.	415 Green St., two doors north of intersection with North Street

SUNDAY
OCTOBER 17, 1965

Early morning	Roxie discovers that Olene hasn't come home from the night before.	Emberton home
Mid morning	Floyd Emberton finds Olene's car.	Two doors north of intersection at Green and North Streets on east side of street
10:00 a.m.	Floyd and Roxie Emberton call police to report Olene's disappearance.	Emberton home
10:15 a.m.	Police respond to call and start talking to Olene's friends.	
Mid-day	Friends from the Emberton's church visit the family to offer prayers and support.	Emberton home
Afternoon	Floyd Emberton threatens Tom Preston, and Sheriff Grimme responds by placing Tom under protective custody.	Emberton home

MONDAY
OCTOBER 18, 1965

8:00 a.m.	Tipton High School students start their new week. Very few know Olene is missing.	Tipton High School
2:00 p.m. (Est.)	Mrs. Don Clouser discovers Olene's body lying next to a cornfield near her farm.	Northeast Tipton County between Windfall and Hobbs
2:10 p.m. (Est.)	Larry Clouser phones the sheriff's office to report Olene's body, but the dispatcher misunderstands and assumes Olene is alive.	Clouser farm in northeast Tipton County

MONDAY
OCTOBER 18, 1965 — continued

2:15 p.m.	Dispatcher puts out call: "What you've been looking for has been found."	
2:15 p.m. (Est.)	Grimme is meeting with local and county officials to dust Olene's car for fingerprints. He hears dispatcher's call and responds.	Intersection of Green and North Streets
2:30 p.m. (Est.)	Grimme arrives at site where Olene's body was found; calls Trooper Robert Zell to the scene. Phil Nichols, driving Young-Nichols ambulance, also arrives.	County Road 450, a half mile north of Division Road on Clouser farm
3:00 p.m. (Est.)	Principal Charles Edwards announces delay of school dismissal and calls several students to his office for questioning by Sheriff Grimme.	Tipton High School
4:30 p.m. (Est.)	Phil Nichols drops off Olene's body at Leatherman-Morris Funeral Home for autopsy performed by Dr. James McFadden of Lafayette.	Leatherman-Morris Funeral Home, 314 N. Main St.
Evening	Friends of Olene's family gather at the Emberton home to express condolences and show support.	Emberton home

TUESDAY
OCTOBER 19, 1965   News of Olene's death is announced in papers throughout Indiana. They report that 48 to 72 hours are required to determine the autopsy findings.

TUESDAY
OCTOBER 19, 1965 — continued

Mid morning	Sheriff Grimme and state police officers conduct a morning press conference.	Sheriff's office

WEDNESDAY
OCTOBER 20, 1965

Early morning	Press briefing: although the investigation has expanded into all surrounding counties, nothing new has been found.	Sheriff's office
Mid morning	Principal Charles Edwards leads a procession of about 75 of Olene's friends and classmates from the school to the funeral home to say goodbye and express condolences to her family.	From Tipton High School to Leatherman-Morris Funeral Home
Mid afternoon	*Tipton Tribune* quotes local law enforcement officers that the case is at a "standstill" pending autopsy and toxicology reports.	
4:00 p.m.	Olene's funeral, conducted by the Rev. Eulon Knox, former minister of Tipton's Church of Christ, is held.	Leatherman-Morris Funeral Home

THURSDAY
OCTOBER 21, 1965

Statewide, newspapers report that progress on the case depends on the arrival of the autopsy report.

FRIDAY
OCTOBER 29, 1965

Mid morning	Sheriff Grimme receives autopsy report. He issues a bulletin and calls a press conference to announce the official cause of death: Undetermined.

TUESDAY
NOVEMBER 23, 1965   The *Tipton Tribune* runs a story announcing that the Emberton family and the local union of the United Steelworkers have hired Pinkerton Detective Agency.

WEDNESDAY
NOVEMBER 24, 1965   The *Kokomo Tribune* announces that it is offering a $500 reward to any private individual with information that solves the case.

FRIDAY
NOVEMBER 26, 1965   The *Tipton Tribune* reports that the state police had administered lie detector tests to Olene's father, Floyd, and her oldest brother, Floyd Wayne. Sheriff Grimme wouldn't talk about the results, but since no arrests were made, it can be assumed that any suspicions about the Embertons were cleared by the tests.

WEDNESDAY
FEBRUARY 16, 1966   Floyd and Roxie announce that they are offering a $5,000 reward for information leading to "the apprehension and conviction of the person or persons responsible for the illegal disposing of Olene Emberton's body along the country road." [This is a misdemeanor in Indiana.]

TUESDAY
NOVEMBER 8, 1966   Verl Grimme easily wins re-election as Tipton County Sheriff, but he is never able to bring the Emberton case to a final resolution.

TUESDAY
OCTOBER 17, 1967   The *Kokomo Morning Times* runs a story reporting that the Emberton family announced their intention to hire a professional investigation agency "in the near future." Floyd is quoted as saying, "I still firmly believe this can be cleared up. I have hope that this will come about soon." No progress in the case was ever reported.

Who's Who

Abney, Wanda Cherry — *member of Tipton High School Class of 1966*

Achenbach, Ed — *friend of Tom Preston and member of Tipton High School Class of 1966*

Berkemeier, Dave — *two-term Tipton mayor, 1992-99*

Blacklidge, Richard H. — *former publisher of* Kokomo Tribune *(deceased)*

Brackney, Bill — *friend of Tom Preston and member of Tipton High School Class of 1966*

Bradley, James — *former Indiana State Police Officer who investigated Perry Steven Miller's 1969 Hamilton County abduction and rape case (deceased)*

Brooks, Patricia Scott — *friend of Olene and member of Tipton High School Class of 1966*

Brown, Karen Sottong — *member of Tipton High School Class of 1966*

Cels, Jennifer Wiggins — *member of Tipton High School Class of 1966*

Clouser, Larry — *farmer who's mother discovered Olene's body (deceased)*

Colgate, Michael — *former Indiana State Police officer and friend of Tipton Sheriff Verl Grimme*

Compton, George — *Tipton physician (deceased)*

Conwell, Terry — *member of Tipton High School Class of 1966*

Cummins, Alice Pitcher — *member of Tipton High School Class of 1966*

Curry, Neal — *friend of Tom Preston and Olene, and member of Tipton High School Class of 1965*

Edgar, Jill Kinder — *member of Tipton High School Class of 1966*

Edwards, Charles — *Tipton High School Principal from 1965 through 1974*

Edwards, Mary — *mother of Trina Edwards, member of Tipton High School Class of 1966 (deceased)*

Edwards, Trina — *member of Tipton High School Class of 1966 (deceased)*

Emberton, Bobby Gene — *Olene's youngest brother who died in a car crash in 1990*

Emberton, David Allen — *Olene's brother (deceased)*

Emberton, Debbie — *Olene's sister-in-law, who married David*

Emberton, Olene — *member of Tipton High School Class of 1966 who died October 17, 1965*

Emberton, Floyd — *Olene's father (deceased)*

Emberton, Floyd Wayne — *Olene's oldest brother*

Emberton, Roxie — *Olene's mother (deceased)*

Essig, Don — *officer of Farmers Loan & Trust (deceased)*

Foland, Sharon Bronson — *member of Tipton High School Class of 1966*

Forney, Robert — *former toxicologist for Indiana University Medical Center (deceased)*

Forney, Jr., Robert — *adjunct associate professor at the College of Pharmacy at the University of Toledo and chief toxicologist for the Lucas County Coroner's Office*

Francis, Earl — *long-time Indiana State Police officer (deceased)*

Gipson, Anna — *member of Tipton High School Class of 1965*

Grimme, Beryl — *brother of former Tipton Sheriffs Verl and Paul Grimme*

Grimme, Paul — *brother of Verl Grimme and Tipton County Sheriff, 1955-58 (deceased)*

Grimme, Verl — *Tipton County Sheriff, 1963-1970, who investigated the Emberton case (deceased)*

Harmon, Jim — *member of Tipton High School Class of 1966*

Havens, Don — *former reporter at* Kokomo Morning Times *and current mayor of Tipton*

Holmes, Horace — *former Tipton County prosecutor, Tipton Circuit Court judge, and attorney in private practice (deceased)*

Horton, Randy — *member of Tipton High School Class of 1966 and former Tipton police officer*

Howard, Jerry — *member of Tipton High School Class of 1965 (deceased)*

Huss, Shirley Stewart — *member of Tipton High School Class of 1966*

Ihnat, Dixie McNew — *member of Tipton High School Class of 1966*

Jay, Marijane Fakes — *member of Tipton High School Class of 1966*

King, Jack — *Tipton man who was shot to death during a card came on July 31, 1955*

Knox, Rev. Eulon — *minister who officiated at Olene's funeral*

Lewis, Sandy McCullough — *member of Tipton High School Class of 1966*

Maddox, Garland — *president of the local Steelworkers (deceased)*

Maney, R.D. — Tipton Tribune *columnist (deceased)*

McFadden, James — *Lafayette-based medical examiner and pathologist, who performed Olene's autopsy (deceased)*

McGaw, Dave — *former Tipton Junior High science teacher and stringer for* Kokomo Morning Times

Merkle, Albert — *former Indiana State Police detective*

Miller, Perry Steven — *friend of Olene and member of Tipton High School Class of 1965*

Mitchell, Chester — *former Tipton County coroner (deceased)*

Moore, Patricia — *long-time Tipton High School guidance counselor (deceased)*

Morris, Doris — *Floyd Emberton's first cousin*

Morris Ted — *officer of Farmers Loan & Trust and Emberton family relative (deceased)*

Murray, Dennis — *member of Tipton High School Class of 1966 (deceased)*

Nangle, Bill — *former editor at* Kokomo Morning Times *(deceased)*

Neuf, Charles E. — *former Illinois State Trooper, LEIU Agent, State Police Detective and author of* State Police Trooper Action Short Stories

Nichols, Brad — *Tipton County coroner*

Nichols, Phil — *former Tipton County coroner (deceased)*

O'Banion, John — *close Emberton family friend and member of Tipton High School Class of 1966*

Overdorf, Clyde — *Tipton County Sheriff 1959-63 (deceased)*

Pinkerton, Allen — *founder of Pinkerton Detective Agency*

Porter, Vickie Sallee — *member of Tipton High School Class of 1966*

Powell, Jo Anna Weber — *member of Tipton High School Class of 1966*

Pratt, James — *former Tipton Police chief 1962-72 (deceased)*

Preston, Tom — *Olene's one-time boyfriend and member of Tipton High School Class of 1966 (deceased)*

Randall, Dr. Brad — *forensic pathologist and author of* Death Investigation: The Basics

Regnier, Richard — *Tipton County prosecutor, 1962-1966 (deceased)*

Reeves, Ann Cain — *member of Tipton High School Class of 1966*

Ripberger, Karen Burk — *member of Tipton High School Class of 1966*

Rogers, Dorman — *former Tipton High School vice principal and later principal (deceased)*

Roseberry, Karyn Harkness — *member of Tipton High School Class of 1966*

Roudebush, Phil — *friend of Olene and member of Tipton High School Class of 1966*

Russell, Mike — *friend of Olene whose wedding she attended the day she went missing (deceased)*

Russell, Mollie Reecer — *friend of Olene whose wedding she attended the day she went missing*

Scelta, Floetta McAdams — *member of Tipton High School Class of 1966*

Shields, Sue — *Hamilton County Circuit Court judge who heard Perry Steven Miller's 1969 kidnapping and rape case. She was the first female judge in Indiana and later served on the Federal bench as a magistrate. (deceased)*

Shoup, Ken — *Tipton High School teacher (deceased)*

Tidler, Bill — *member of Tipton High School Class of 1966*

V.D.M. — *initials of Vincent D. McGraw, head of Pinkerton office in Indianapolis (deceased)*

Watson, Joe — *Tipton attorney who represented the Emberton family*

Wiggins, Mary and Roscoe — *residents of the home on North Green Street next to the spot where Olene's car had been parked (deceased)*

Wilkins, Ron — *former* Tipton Tribune *reporter who covered Steve Miller's 1991 murder trial.*

Wix, Gail Purdue — *member of Tipton High School Class of 1966*

W.R.S. — *initials of Pinkerton detective assigned to investigate Olene's case*

Young, Keith — *first sergeant with the Indiana State Police and technician with the Indiana State Police Crime Lab (deceased)*

Zell, Robert — *former Indiana State Police officer (deceased)*

FICTIONAL CHARACTERS AND CELEBRITIES MENTIONED

Black Dahlia — *the name posthumously assigned to Elizabeth Short, whose brutal 1947 murder in Los Angeles remains unsolved*

Bordon, Lizzie — *suspect in the notorious axe murders of her father and stepmother in Fall River, Massachusetts, in 1892*

Buttram, Pat — *movie and television actor and comedian*

Caputo, Theresa — *reality TV's* Long Island Medium

DuBoise, Allison — *inspiration behind NBC's long-running series* Medium

Fife, Barney — *deputy sheriff character on TV's* Andy Griffith Show

Dalton Gang — *legendary American outlaws*

Haskell, Eddie — *character on TV's* Leave It to Beaver

Hoy, David — *Kentucky-based radio psychic who gained fame in the 1960s and '70s*

Jack the Ripper — *legendary, unidentified serial killer, who stalked his female victims on the streets of London in 1888*

James, Jesse — *legendary American outlaw*

Kilmer, Val — *movie actor*

Lincoln, President Abraham

Rockwell, Norman — *beloved American illustrator and painter*

Roosevelt, President Franklin D.

Sheppard, Dr. Sam — *a surgeon convicted for the 1954 murder of his wife but later acquitted*

Stark, Jim — *name of James Dean's character in classic movie*, Rebel Without a Cause

Taylor, Andy Taylor — *sheriff character on TV's* Andy Griffith *Show*

Van Praagh, James — *psychic author*

Bibliography

NEWSPAPERS

"$5,000 Reward Offered for Good Tips on Olene." Feb. 17, 1966, *Kokomo* (Indiana) *Morning Times*.

"2 Boy Friends of Slain Girl Guarded." Oct. 19, 1965. *Indianapolis* (Indiana) *News*.

"50 Persons Questioned in Tipton Girl's Death." Oct. 20, 1965. *Indianapolis* (Indiana) *News*.

"Additional Charges Filed: Total Bond Set at $80,500 for Perry Steven Miller." May 31, 1969. *Tipton* (Indiana) *Tribune*.

Advertisement: "IMPORTANT! To All Voters of Tipton County." Nov. 4, 1960. *Tipton* (Indiana) *Tribune*.

"Appointed to Park Board." May 29, 1952. *Tipton* (Indiana) *Tribune*.

"Assault Charges Filed Against Tipton Man. May 22, 1969. *Tipton* (Indiana) *Tribune*.

"Assault Suspect to Be Examined by Psychiatrists." June 12, 1969. *Noblesville* (Indiana) *Daily Ledger*.

"Attempted Rape Added to Charge." April 28, 1966. *Tipton* (Indiana) *Tribune*.

"Autopsy Delaying Girl's Death Probe." Oct. 21, 1965. *Indianapolis* (Indiana) *News*.

"Bank Robbed of $8,000 at Sharpsville." Oct. 28, 1966. *Tipton* (Indiana) *Tribune*.

"Bond Reduced in Miller Case." May 6, 1966. *Tipton* (Indiana) *Tribune*.

"Card of Thanks. Oct. 26, 1965. *Tipton* (Indiana) *Tribune*.

"Cause Still Unknown: Police Press Investigation of Tipton Girl's Death." Oct. 21, 1965. *Indianapolis* (Indiana) *Star*.

"Charges Filed Against Tipton Man for Rape." May 24, 1969. *Noblesville* (Indiana) *Daily Ledger*.

"City Desk Memos: Is Tragedy an Awakener?" Oct. 22, 1965. *Indianapolis* (Indiana) *News*.

"City to Have Baseball Team." June 10, 1950. *Tipton* (Indiana) *Tribune*.

"Clues Fail to Check out in Emberton Case." Nov. 3, 1965. *Tipton* (Indiana) *Tribune*.

"Clues Sought in Local Slaying." Oct. 19, 1965. *Tipton* (Indiana) *Tribune*.

"Court News." May 12, 1966. *Elwood* (Indiana) *Call-Leader*.

"Court News." Sept. 28, 1966. *Tipton* (Indiana) *Tribune*.

"Death of Olene One Year Ago Is Still a Mystery." Oct. 15, 1966. *Kokomo* (Indiana) *Morning Times*.

"Death Penalty Asked for Three." Nov. 20, 1990. *The Vidette-Messenger* (Porter County, Indiana).

"Defense: Wood Saving Self." April 10, 1991. *The Vidette-Messenger* (Porter County, Indiana).

"Deputy Sheriff Gets Aching Head from Encased Arm." April 22, 1955. *Tipton* (Indiana) *Tribune.*

"Directors Rename Grimme Head of Youth Foundation." Jan. 30, 1957. *Tipton* (Indiana) *Tribune.*

"Emberton Case: $5,000 Reward Offered." Feb. 16, 1966. *Kokomo* (Indiana) *Tribune.*

"Emberton Death Mystery Moves into Second Year." Oct. 18, 1966. *Kokomo* (Indiana) *Tribune.*

"Emberton Fund Gets Donations." Nov. 29, 1965. *Kokomo (Indiana) Morning Times.*

"Embertons Discuss Case: 48 Days Since Olene Seen Alive, Trail Cold." Dec. 3, 1965. *Kokomo* (Indiana) *Tribune.*

"Escapees Quietly Caught on Trimble Farm." Feb. 9, 1956. *Tipton* (Indiana) *Tribune.*

"Ex-convict's Early Release a Mistake." Nov. 26, 1990. *Kokomo* (Indiana) *Tribune.*

"Expect Medical Report on Tipton Girl Very Soon." Oct. 29, 1965. *Kokomo* (Indiana) *Morning Times.*

"Father Plans Private Investigation on 2nd Anniversary of Emberton's Death." Oct. 17, 1967. *Kokomo* (Tribune) *Morning Times.*

"Father, Union Hire Detective Firm." Nov. 24, 1965. *Kokomo* (Indiana) *Morning Times.*

"Flying Saucer Spotted Sunday in Tipton County." May 18, 1964. *Tipton (Indiana) Tribune.*

"Funds Requested for Financing Probe of Death." Nov. 24, 1965. *Tipton* (Indiana) *Tribune.*

"Girl Missing from Home. Oct. 18, 1965." *Tipton* (Indiana) *Tribune.*

"Graduation Night Will Be Sad to Tipton's Emberton Family." May 25, 1966. *Tipton* (Indiana) *Tribune.*

"Grimme Is Promoted." Sept. 22, 1944, *Tipton* (Indiana) *Tribune.*

"Grimme Loses Teeth in Baseball Mishap." Sept. 28, 1933. *Tipton* (Indiana) *Tribune.*

"Group to Discuss Kids' Softball, Baseball Loop." Feb. 25, 1953. *Tipton* (Indiana) *Tribune.*

"Guilty on 4 Counts: Perry Miller Nets Life Sentence." Sept. 17, 1969. *Tipton* (Indiana) *Tribune.*

"High School Stunned: Tipton Students Pay Last Respects to Olene."

Oct. 20, 1965. *Kokomo* (Indiana) *Tribune*.

"Hobbs Crash Fatal to City Youth: Thomas Preston Injured Fatally in Midnight Mishap." June 9, 1966. *Tipton* (Indiana) *Tribune*.

"In Madison County: Miller Charged With Kidnap." May 28, 1969. *Tipton* (Indiana) *Tribune*.

"In Memoriam." Oct. 17, 1966. *Tipton* (Indiana) *Tribune*.

"Is Transferred. "July 29, 1942. *Tipton* (Indiana) *Tribune*.

"It's Death for Miller." May 20, 1991. *The Vidette-Messenger* (Porter County, Indiana).

"Last Witness Called in Miller Trial." Sept. 15, 1969. *Tipton* (Indiana) *Tribune*.

"Lead 'Falls Flat' in Tipton Girl's Death Case." Oct. 23, 1965. *Indianapolis* (Indiana) *Star*.

"Legion Names Committee Heads." June 19, 1951. *Tipton* (Indiana) *Tribune*.

"Lie Detector Tests Given in Emberton Case." Nov. 26, 1965. *Tipton* (Indiana) *Tribune*.

"Little New about Death of Tipton Girl." Oct. 22 1965. *Kokomo* (Indiana) *Morning Times*.

"M/Sgt. Grimme, Member of Third Air Division." Feb. 8, 1945. *Tipton* (Indiana) *ribune*.

"Man Gets 138 Years in Murder of Clerk." Aug. 9, 2001. *Indianapolis* (Indiana) *Star*.

"Meteor Fragments Found in County." Sept. 20, 1966. *Tipton* (Indiana) *Tribune*.

"Miller Faces New Charges in Madison Co." May 28, 1969. *Noblesville* (Indiana) *Daily Ledger*.

"Miller Gets Life Sentence." Oct. 9, 1969. *Tipton* (Indiana) *Tribune*.

"Miller Says New Trial Necessary." June 21, 1991. *The Vidette-Messenger* (Porter County, Indiana).

"Missing Purse Link in Tipton Mystery." Oct. 20, 1965. *Kokomo* (Indiana) *Tribune*.

"Missing Tipton Girl's Body Found in Ditch." Oct. 19, 1965. *Indianapolis* (Indiana) *Star*.

"Murder Suspects Back in County." Nov. 17, 1990. *The Vidette-Messenger* (Porter County, Indiana).

"Mysterious Tipton Death Report Due." Oct. 27, 1965. *Indianapolis* (Indiana) *News*.

"Mystery Case Hinges on Lab Tests." Oct. 21, 1965. *Kokomo* (Indiana) *Tribune*.

"Newly Elected County Officers Take Oath." Jan. 7, 1955. *Tipton* (Indiana)

Tribune.

"No Official Cause of Tipton Girl's Death Can Be Found." Oct. 29, 1965. *Kokomo* (Indiana) *Tribune.*

"Nothing New in Emberton Case." Nov. 18, 1965. *Tipton* (Indiana) *Tribune.*

"Olene Wanted to Be Teacher, but Death Snuffed Her Dreams." Nov. 22, 1965. *Kokomo* (Indiana) *Morning Times.*

"Olene's Birthday: This Was to Be Special Day in One Tipton Home." Dec. 17, 1965. *Kokomo* (Indiana) *Tribune.*

"Pathologist Discusses Emberton Case; Lists Unexplained Deaths." Dec. 7, 1965. *Kokomo* (Indiana) *Tribune.*

"Phyllis LaGarde, Verl Grimme Exchange Vows." July 17, 1948. *Tipton* (Indiana) *Tribune.*

"Pinkerton's to Join Probe in Emberton Case." Nov. 23, 1965. *Tipton* (Indiana) *Tribune.*

"Plans in Making for Softball League to Open Next Month." May 24, 1950. *Tipton* (Indiana) *Tribune.*

"Police Believe Murder Case Solved." Nov. 16. 1990. *The Vidette-Messenger* (Porter County, Indiana).

"Prairie." July 16, 1942. *Tipton* (Indiana) *Tribune.*

"Promotion." April 28, 1943. *Tipton* (Indiana) *Tribune.*

"Prosecutor Says Wood Too Dumb to Lie: Perry Miller Fate in Hands of Jurors." April 17, 1991. *The Vidette-Messenger* (Porter County, Indiana).

"Pulaski Jury Finds Miller Guilty of Murder, Rape." April 18, 1991. *Logansport* (Indiana) *Pharos-Tribune.*

"Pupils Pay Respects to Girl; Case at Standstill Pending Report on Autopsy." Oct. 20, 1965. *Tipton* (Indiana) *Tribune.*

"Republicans Unseat Four in County." Nov. 7, 1962. *Tipton* (Indiana) *Tribune.*

"Reward for Information in Emberton Case." Feb. 16, 1966. *Tipton* (Indiana) *Tribune.*

"Round Town with the *Tribune.*" Feb. 7, 1951. *Tipton* (Indiana) *Tribune.*

"Round Town with the *Tribune.*" Oct. 28, 1965. *Tipton* (Indiana) *Tribune.*

"Ruling Is Awaited on Death Cause." Oct. 22, 1965. *Indianapolis* (Indiana) *News.*

"Rumors Abound but Just Talk, Reports Sheriff." Jan. 12, 1966. *Tipton* (Indiana) *Tribune.*

"Sergeants Leonard, Verl Grimme Home from Germany." July 6, 1945. *Tipton* (Indiana) *Tribune.*

"Seven Tipton Youths Queried on Vandalism." April 4, 1957. *Tipton*

(Indiana) *Tribune*.
"Sheriff Candidate." May 3, 1962. Tipton (Indiana) *Tribune*.
"Sheriff Seeks More Speed on Laboratory Tests." Oct. 22, 1965. Kokomo (Indiana) *Tribune*.
"Sheriff Stymied on Tipton Death." Nov. 4, 1965. Kokomo (Indiana) *Morning Times*.
"Sheriff's Department Apprehends Kokomo Robbers on U.S. 31." Aug. 28, 1970. Tipton (Indiana) *Tribune*.
"State Presents Case: Steven P. Miller Trial to Reach Jury Today." Sept. 12, 1969. Tipton (Indiana) T*ribune*.
"Stepfather Now in Custody." Nov. 18, 1990. The *Vidette-Messenger* (Porter County, Indiana).
"Still No New Clues in Tipton Girl's Death." Oct. 25, 1965. Kokomo (Tribune) *Tribune*.
"Store Clerk Is Missing." Nov. 14, 1990. *The Vidette-Messenger* (Porter County, Indiana).
"Superior Court Scene as Jury Trial Begins." Sept. 8, 1969. Noblesville (Indiana) *Daily Ledger*.
"Teen Says Miller Was There." April 9, 1991. The *Vidette-Messenger* (Porter County, Indiana).
"Tests Today May Show Cause of Girl's Death." Oct. 20, 1965. *Indianapolis* (Indiana) *Star*.
"Three Sons in Service." Sept. 2, 1941. Tipton (Indiana) *Tribune*.
"Three Under Arrest in Rape Case." May 23, 1969. Noblesville (Indiana) *Daily Ledger*.
"Tipton Case No Nearer Solving After 12 Days." Oct. 28, 1965. Kokomo (Indiana) *Tribune*.
"Tipton Death Remains Mystery; 2 Released." Oct. 21, 1965. Kokomo (Indiana) *Morning Times*.
"Tipton Death Still a Mystery." Oct. 19, 1965. Kokomo (Indiana) *Tribune*.
"Tipton Girl Missing After Teen Party." Oct. 18, 1965. Kokomo (Indiana) *Tribune*.
"Tipton Girl's Death Defies Explanation." Oct. 20, 1965. Muncie (Indiana) *Evening Press*.
"Tipton Girl's Nude Body Is Found." Oct. 19, 1965. Kokomo (Indiana) *Morning Times*.
"Tipton Man Charged in Rape of Elwood Girl." May 31, 1969. *Anderson* (Indiana) *Daily Bulletin*.
"Tipton Man Charged with Kidnap, Rape." May 30, 1969. Kokomo (Indiana) *Tribune*.
"Tipton Man Charged with Kidnapping." May 28, 1969. *Elwood* (Indiana)

Call-Leader
"Tipton Sheriff Checks 'Good Lead.' " Oct. 22, 1965. *Indianapolis* (Indiana) *Star.*
"Tipton Youth Admits Attempted Rape." April 28, 1966. Page 3. *Kokomo* (Indiana) *Tribune.*
"Trial by Jury Tops Cases in Circuit Court." May 17, 1966. *Tipton* (Indiana) *Tribune.*
"*Tribune* Offers Reward of $500." Nov. 24, 1965. *Kokomo* (Indiana) *Tribune.*
"Truck Loaded with Popcorn Overturns." June 7, 1955. *Tipton* (Indiana) *Tribune.*
"Two Brothers Meet in England, Then Locate a Cousin." Sept. 30, 1944. *Tipton* (Indiana) *Tribune.*
"Victim: Murder Suspect Should Not Have Been Paroled." April 13, 1991. *Tipton* (Indiana) *Tribune.*
"What Happened to Olene? Case Appears at Dead End as Investigation Drags on." Nov. 30, 1965. *Kokomo* (Indiana) *Tribune.*
"Winter Claims 1st Casualty in Tipton County." Jan. 24, 1965. *Tipton* (Indiana) *Tribune.*
"Withdraws Plea of 'Not Guilty.' " Nov. 29, 1966. *Tipton* (Indiana) *Tribune.*
"WLS PROGRAM — Cast for Prairie Entertainment Is Announced." Jan. 19, 1942." *Tipton* (Indiana) *Tribune.*

BOOK
State Police Trooper Action Short Stories About Daily Encounters, Chases, Crashes, Riots & Investigations of Murder & Theft. Neuf, Charles E. Published by the author. 2011.

MAGAZINES
Newsweek, Nov. 12, 2015, about $20 million program about psychics "to visualize hidden extremist training sites."
"An Evaluation of Remote Viewing: Research and Applications" — C.I.A. Report 1995.
"Use of Psychics in Law Enforcement" … a 1998 Report.
May 1979 edition of The Police Chief ran an article titled, "Managing the Psychic in Criminal investigations."

WEB
Medscape
https://emedicine.medscape.com/article/1785357-overview#showall
IN.gov (Indiana State Coroners Training Board)
http://www.in.gov/ctb/2328.htm

PERSONAL & EMAIL INTERVIEWS

Abney, Wanda Cherry — 2016
Achenbach, Ed — 2016
Berkemeier, Dave — 2017
Brackney, Bill — 2007
Bradley, James — 2006
Brooks, Patricia Scott — 2017
Brown, Karen Sottong — 2017
Cels, Jennifer Wiggins — 2017
Coan, Mary Neal — 2017
Colgate, Michael — 2006
Conwell, Terry — 2017
Cummins, Alice Pitcher — 2016
Curry, Neal — 2010, 2017
Edgar, Jill Kinder — 2017
Edwards, Charles — 2005
Emberton, Debbie — 2016, 2018
Foland, Sharon Bronson — 2017
Forney, Robert Jr. — 2004
Gipson, Anna — 2016
Grimme, Beryl — 2005
Harmon, Jim — 2017
Hart, Dick — 2006
Horton, Randy — 2017
Huss, Shirley Stewart — 2016
Ihnat, Dixie McNew — 2016
Jay, Marijane Fakes — 2017
Lewis, Sandy McCullough — 2017
Littlejohn, Justus — 2006
Morris, Doris — 2017, 2018
Murray, Dennis — 2005
Nichols, Brad — 2018
Nichols, Phil — 2005
O'Banion, John — 2017
Peters, Linda Stewart — 2016
Porter, Keith — 2004
Porter, Vickie Sallee — 2017
Powell, Jo Anna Weber — 2016
Pratt, James — 2006
Reeves, Ann Cain — 2016
Ripberger, Karen Burk — 2017
Roudebush, Phillip — 2018
Roseberry, Karyn Harkness — 2016
Russell, Mollie Reecer — 2017
Scelta, Floetta McAdams — 2017
Talbert, Marshall "Marty" — 2017, 2018
Tarrh, Mike — 2018
Tidler, William E. — 2017
Watson, Joe — 2016
Wittkamper, Marla Henderson — 2017
Wix, Gail Perdue — 2016
Zell, Robert — 2006

Index

Abney, Wanda Cherry, *32, 92, 110*
Achenbach, Ed, *24, 33, 98, 123*
Ball State University, *7, 31*
Berkemeier, Dave, *95-6*
Blacklidge, Richard H., *114*
Brackney, Bill, *97*
Bradley, James, *138-9*
Brigg's Restaurant, *53*
Brooks, Patricia Scott, *23, 36, 56, 154*
Brown, Karen Sottong, *58*
Carter's Grocery, *102*
Cels, Jennifer Wiggins, *31, 53, 55, 58, 84, 101, 116-8, 146, 155*
Church of Christ, *7, 23, 36, 42, 162, 165*
Clinton County, *65*
Clouser, Larry, *6, 14, 19, 80, 163-4*
Coan, Mary Neal, *35, 101*
Colgate, Michael, *5, 76, 83, 95*
Compton, George, *72*
Conwell, Terry, *57, 59, 63, 91, 101, 155*
Cummins, Alice Pitcher, *29, 32*
Curry, Neal, *93, 99-101*
Diana Theatre, *xv, 10-1, 99, 109, 160, 162*
Edgar, Jill Kinder, *32, 92, 102, 153-4*
Edwards, Charles, *xiii, xiv, 2, 25-6, 54, 59, 98, 107, 164-5*
Edwards, Mary, *92*
Edwards, Trina, *92*
Elwood, *135-6, 148*
Emberton, Bobby Gene, *27, 30, 41-2, 46, 151*
Emberton, David, *29, 30, 42-3, 46, 151*
Emberton, Debbie, *ix, xviii, xx, 42-4, 96, 144, 148*
Emberton, Floyd, *5, 22, 24-5, 30, 34, 36-47, 55, 59, 65, 89-90, 95, 97-9, 112, 116, 125-7, 152, 155, 163, 166*
Emberton, Floyd Wayne, *3, 12-3, 30, 37-8, 42, 46, 90, 151, 162, 166*
Emberton, Roxie, *5, 7, 11-2, 22, 29, 30, 36-47, 55-6, 59, 62-3, 95-7, 112, 115-6, 123, 125-7, 139, 140, 144, 155, 162-3, 166*
Essig, Don, *113*
Farmers Loan & Trust, *46, 113, 126*
Foland, Sharon Bronson, *101, 154*
Forney, Robert Jr., *73*
Foster's Jewelry Store, *85*
Francis, Earl, *52*
Gipson, Anna, *92*
Grimme, Beryl, *76-7, 81-2, 85*
Grimme, Verl, *xiii, 5-6, 14, 23-4, 26, 52-3, 65-9, 72, 74-87, 90-1, 93-5, 112-3, 115-6, 118-21, 123-4, 126-7, 129, 132-3, 136, 141, 144, 148, 150-3, 163-6*
Hamilton County, *65, 135-6, 138-9*
Harmon, Jim, *34-5, 154-5,*
Havens, Don, *xi-xii, 150*
Hendricks County Hospital, *48, 121*
Hobbs, *5, 77, 80, 102, 105, 120, 128, 163*
Horton, Randy, *33, 74, 82-3, 86, 102, 153*
Howard County, *18, 44, 65, 113, 139*
Howard, Jerry, *109*
Huss, Shirley Stewart, *54, 58, 102*
Ihnat, Dixie McNew, *84, 92, 101*
Indiana State Police Crime Lab, *50, 66, 68, 122, 124,*
Indiana State Prison, *137-9*
Indiana University Health-Ball Memorial Hospital, *50*
Indiana University Medical Center, *50,*

66, 68, 73
Jackson, Olean, *xiii*, 36, 45, 156
Jay, Marijane Fakes, *101*
Jefferson School, *xix*, *10*, *30*, *32*, *34-5*
Jim Dandy Drive-in, *2*, *27*
King, Jack, *85*
Leatherman-Morris Funeral Home, 48, 50, 54, 61, 164-5
Lewis, Sandy McCullough, *101*
Lincoln School, *30*, *32-3*
Littlejohn, Justus, *124*
Lutheran School, *10*
Madison County, *65*
Maddox, Garland, *113*
McFadden, James, *48-50, 52, 72-4, 121, 164*
McGaw, Dave, *152*
McIntosh, Louise, *2*
Merkle, Albert, *72*
Miller, Perry Steven, *128-41, 160*
Mitchell, Chester, *70, 72, 87, 119*
Moore, Patricia, *26*
Morris, Doris, *34, 36-7, 45-7, 59, 126, 155, 156*
Morris, Ted, *113, 126*
Murray, Dennis, *32-3*
Nangle, Bill, *150*
Nichols, Brad, 50, *73*
Nichols, Phil, *14-5, 27, 164*
O'Banion, John, *3, 27, 37-42, 44*
Physicians Clinical Lab, *48, 121*
Pinkerton Detective Agency, *112-8, 121, 123, 126, 166*
Porter County, *44, 137, 139*
Porter, Keith, *61-2*
Porter, Vickie Sallee, *31, 55, 57, 91, 102*
Powell, Jo Anna Weber, *32-4, 55-6, 58-9, 63, 97, 102-3*

Pratt, James, 5, 6, 22, 48-50, 52, 66, 72, 82, 88, 93-4, 103-5, 131-2
Preston, Tom, *24-5, 27, 32, 40-1, 81, 94, 97-111, 119, 160, 163*
Reeves, Ann Cain, *26-7, 34, 58, 84, 91, 101-2*
Regnier, Richard, *5, 20, 72, 113, 116, 118-9, 123, 138, 156*
Ripberger, Karen Burk, *32*
Rogers, Dorman, *31*
Roseberry, Karyn Harkness, *32, 92-3, 109*
Roudebush, Phil, *10-3, 22-4, 52, 162*
Russell, Mike, 7, 9, 23, 162
Russell, Molly Reecer, *7, 9, 10, 23, 36, 162*
Scelta, Floetta McAdams, *54, 56, 87, 92, 103, 155*
Six-Acres Drive-in, *xv*, *12*
Smith, Margaret, *85*
St. John's Catholic School, *103, 107*
Talbert, Marshall "Marty," *18-21, 29, 44-5, 113, 130, 139-140*
Tarrh, Mike, *140-1*
Tidler, William E., *55-6*
Tipton County Memorial Hospital, *3, 34, 47, 72, 131,*
Tipton High School, *xiii, xiv, xvi, 24-5, 30-1, 36, 51, 54, 60, 97-8, 107, 129, 130, 163-5*
Tompkinsville, Kentucky, *29, 45-6*
Tom's Cafeteria, *9, 162*
Watson, Joe, *85-6, 126, 144*
Wix, Gail Perdue, *2, 25, 32, 54-5, 58, 92, 98-9, 108, 153, 155*
Young-Nichols Funeral Home, *3, 6, 14, 27, 48, 50, 119, 164*
Zell, Robert, *15-7, 52, 69, 75-6, 85, 90, 94, 103-4, 164*

HELP KEEP OLENE'S MEMORY ALIVE BY GIVING TO THE OLENE EMBERTON MEMORIAL SCHOLARSHIP FUND

Olene Emberton dreamed of attending college after high school to pursue a career in teaching. Unfortuntaely, when we lost Olene, the world lost the gifts and passions she longed to contribute. But now, through the Tipton County Foundation, there is a way for us to breathe renewed life into the dream Olene was never able to pursue.

The Foundation has offered its expertise and resources to raise funds to benefit Tipton High School graduates embarking on their own journey to a teaching career. This effort would establish a permanent Olene Emberton Memorial Scholarship Fund to provide a $1,000 award each year to such a student.

To attain that goal, we must raise $25,000 by the end of 2018. If the fundraising falls short, whatever amount is received will be utilized for another form of memorial to benefit Olene's alma mater. Regardless of the amount donated, very dollar donated in Olene's name will go toward making a difference in the lives of Tipton High School students enriching the lives of students, who, like her, wish to make a difference in the lives of others.

To make a gift in Olene's memory, please visit *www.tiptoncf.org* or call the Tipton County Foundation at (765) 675-1940. Donations are tax deductible, and any amount will be greatly appreciated.

Thank you.

Wanda Cherry Abney, Dixie McNew Ihnat, and Janis Thornton
Members of the Tipton High School Class of 1966

The Tipton County Foundation is a volunteer-driven nonprofit public charity established in 1986 to serve donors, award grants and scholarships, and provide leadership to improve the quality of life in Tipton County, forever.

About the Author

JANIS THORNTON is a home-grown Tipton author, whose works include two pictorial history books, *Images of America: Tipton County, Indiana* and *Images of America: Frankfort, Indiana*, as well as two cozy mysteries in the "Elmwood Confidential" series, *Dust Bunnies & Dead Bodies* and *Dead Air & Doubles Dares*. She attended school with Olene Emberton and devoted years to researching her tragic death. Visit Janis online at *www.janis-thornton.com*.

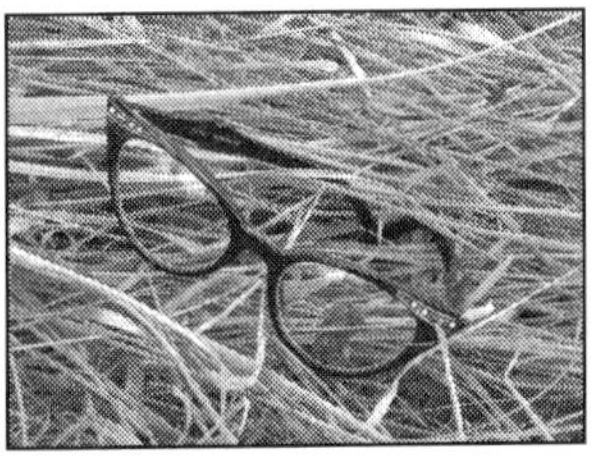